Stanislaw Lem

RECOGNITIONS

detective/suspense
Bruce Cassiday, General Editor

Victorian Masters of Mystery by Audrey Peterson
Roots of Detection edited by Bruce Cassiday
Raymond Chandler by Jerry Speir
P. D. James by Norma Siebenheller
John D. MacDonald by David Geherin
Ross Macdonald by Jerry Speir
The Murder Mystique: Crime Writers on Their Art
edited by Lucy Freeman
Dorothy L. Sayers by Dawson Gaillard
Sons of Sam Spade: The Private Eye Novel in the 70s
by David Geherin

science fiction/fantasy
Sharon Jarvis, General Editor

Fritz Leiber by Tom Staicar
Isaac Asimov by Jean Fiedler and Jim Mele
Ray Bradbury by Wayne L. Johnson
Critical Encounters: Writers and Themes in Science Fiction
edited by Dick Riley
Critical Encounters II: Writers and Themes in Science Fiction
edited by Tom Staicar
The Feminine Eye: Science Fiction and the Women Who Write It
edited by Tom Staicar
Frank Herbert by Timothy O'Reilly
Ursula K. LeGuin by Barbara J. Bucknall
Theodore Sturgeon by Lucy Menger

Also of Interest
The Bedside, Bathtub & Armchair Companion to Agatha Christie
edited by Dick Riley and Pam McAllister
Introduction by Julian Symons

Stanislaw Lem

Richard E. Ziegfeld

Frederick Ungar Publishing Co.
New York

Ziegfeld, Richard E.
  Stanislaw Lem.

  Bibliography: p.
  Includes index.
  1. Lem, Stanislaw.   2. Authors, Polish—20th century—
Biography.   I. Title.
PG7158.L392Z53   1985   891.8′537   83-18009
ISBN 0-8044-2994-4
ISBN 0-8044-6992-X (pbk.)

Table of Contents

Preface

This is, perhaps, the first full-length book on Stanislaw Lem in the English language. It is not, however, an exhaustive, scholarly interpretation of Lem's books. Instead, readers will get an overview of his career, biographical background, an indication of what the key books are about, and a survey of the major themes and literary techniques.

I have raised issues about Lem's work while fully aware that individual topics merit whole chapters in a book. A brief list of possible concerns for scholars might include these items: Analysis of the untranslated material, both fiction and theoretical titles; attention to the newly translated titles as they appear in English; thematic studies on topics such as cybernetics, chance, and Lem's use of science; and studies on his literary technique, discussing narrative persona, formal experimentation, satire, style, and symbols for communication.

The bibliography in this book is extensive but not definitive. It includes information on Polish publication of Lem's books and on most English-language material through 1982 but nothing on foreign-language criticism or foreign-language reception. I have been unable to verify several English-language citations on articles by and about Lem; rather than risk fostering "ghost" bibliographical entries I have omitted them.

At the beginning of each chapter I have cited two dates. The first refers to Polish publication on the original edition. The second date indicates year of American publication.

A number of people have been helpful during the years I

have devoted to the Lem "obsession." My thanks go to Helen Wolff and Grace Budd at Helen and Kurt Wolff Books. They have believed in Lem and have made the preparation of this book a much more pleasant task by furnishing copies of manuscripts that have not yet been published, providing information on Lem, and facilitating contact with his supporters. Dick Riley, then editor at Frederick Ungar, agreed with me that Lem deserved more attention; Larry Zuckerman and Sharon Jarvis tightened the manuscript. Ina Rae Hark and John Ower read and helped hone an early chapter. Olga Amsterdamska and Gene Moore shared my enthusiasm about Lem when very few American university faculty members knew his name. Neil Barron and Hal Hall helped me locate citations in the small science-fiction journals. Finally, Lem himself assisted on several factual matters and offered a helpful critique of the manuscript.

Two people merit special thanks. Paulette Ziegfeld freed me to write and was supportive when "the gods" chose the years between 1979 and 1982 as the time to thrust numerous unpleasant obstacles in my path. And last I want to single out Franz Rottensteiner, who replied to questions with copious detail, persuaded Lem to answer biographical questions, and shared his vast archive of bibliographical information as I labored to straighten out a complicated bibliography and publication history. He furnished information on Lem's book sales, faithfully alerted me to forthcoming publications by or about Lem, and, most significantly, before I could ask, he offered to read the manuscript of this book—all this for a person he did not know and has never met. Every literary artist should have an agent and friend like Franz Rottensteiner.

R.E.Z.

January 15, 1983

Introduction

Stanislaw Lem is truly a Renaissance man. He finished medical school, he has worked as a scientific research assistant, and he is author of one of the most varied bodies of writing in the history of literature. He has studied and is able to write authoritatively about innumerable topics. He is intimately familiar with several foreign cultures (especially American folkways). He is able to read four modern foreign languages and regularly slips Latin phrases into his writing. He has published successful books in more genres than most literate readers could name.

Michael Kandel, critic and widely respected translator of Lem's works, has said that Lem is a "writer of great diversity" yet one "haunted by . . . only a few fundamental ideas." It is true that the same core ideas come up repeatedly in different form and accompanied by evolving detail. But a list of Lem's "few fundamental ideas" is staggering in the scope and the number of his concerns. He regularly raises the subject of the individual and his relationship to other men, to the universe, to other nonhuman civilizations, to space, and to machines. He is just as likely, however, to worry over bureaucracy, the military, communication, mysterious phenomena, biological evolution, particle theory, and the origin of the universe. Space travel, statistical probability, generic theory, the state of Western science fiction, and philosophical theories on God, epistemology, and ethics are also major concerns.

Lem's basic views have not changed radically over the years (except with respect to his optimism). However, he has been so prolific that certain ideas cannot help but show up repeatedly. Perhaps this is why Kandel has been lured into the impression that Lem has only a few fundamental ideas. But with three or four exceptions, each book is so diverse intellectually that reading a Lem novel is like enrolling in one of those infamous surveys of Western civilization: they make a serious attempt in fourteen weeks to summarize the two-thousand-year history of a people. The difference is that Lem provides skillful mastery over every subject as few teachers in such courses do.

Stylistic diversity, generic range, and a flair for the intellectual overview characterize Lem's work. Just as important is the fact that he combines great intelligence and learning with a provocative sense of ambivalence. The ambivalence drives him into an ironic stance from which he seeks to observe and analyze every facet of a problem. Thus, Lem provides a vast intellectual feast. To make this feast manageable to the reader, this book has two strategies. The first is a clear, simple overview of his career through 1982. Within individual chapters, it refers to five elements: a plot precis and discussion of plot, theme, characterization technique, and symbolism. Where appropriate, special attention is paid to critical problems with each book. Finally, comparison is used to evaluate the place of each book in the Lem corpus.

Second, this book's critical approach to Lem's work is the type about which Richard Howard wrote in *Alone with America*. He argued, after his mentor, Auden, that the only truly useful literary criticism is advocacy. This critical stance advances the work of a writer with whom a reader is not familiar or presses forward a little-known portion of an acknowledged master's corpus. At points where Lem's work may not appeal to certain readers, there is an obligation to offer a candid report on those potential difficulties. Nevertheless, the goal is to share a sense of enthusiasm about Lem's virtues and, in the process, to assist in facilitating greater American awareness that Stanislaw Lem is one of the outstanding writers in twentieth-century letters.

Stanislaw Lem

1

The Marginal Man:

Biography

Most of Stanislaw Lem's adult attitudes and literary concerns surfaced during his childhood in Poland before the Nazi occupation. He has written charmingly about this phase of his life in an autobiography called *Wyzoki Żamek* (*High Castle*, untranslated). *High Castle* powerfully recreates his frame of mind and the detail of incidents that shaped his life; however, the book is strikingly devoid of the external detail normally included in biographies, such as names, dates, and locations. Lem treats autobiography as a form of speculative fiction, through which the adult Lem mulls questions concerning a child's version of reality and history—beginning the book, for example, by noting that he is a Lilliputian. The unusual tenor of the autobiography becomes most obvious when he says that he offers insignificant details because they seem more interesting than later memories of the facts and that he finds it easier to speak of circumstances in his childhood than of people. Hence, an account of Lem's life will provide a limited amount of traditional biographical material.

Lem was born September 12, 1921, into a medical family in Lvov, Poland. Both his father and uncle were doctors. He does not speak frequently of his father, Samuel Lem, but clearly he was a significant influence in his life. Of his mother, Sabina (née Wollner), he says virtually nothing. Lem has no siblings.

Lem's earliest memories are of books, chiefly science and literature, and of his father's medical waiting room in one portion of their apartment. These twin interests in science and lit-

erature have dominated his life. He recalls having been
fascinated by his father's anatomy books, even when he was
very small. He was equally fascinated with the purity and precision of signs. Other aspects of his youthful personality,
though, did not augur a bright future in science, where attention to detail and process are critical. He notes, for example,
that during his adolescence he had difficulty distinguishing the
morning from the evening (a fairly severe handicap for a bud-
ding scientist) and that he exhibited little desire, when as-
signed classroom experiments, to follow them through
patiently.

In talking of his childhood, he describes himself as a "monster" who was frequently sick and who loved food—especially
visits to the chocolate and pastry shops—so much that culinary
images pervade this stage of his life. He had many acquaint-
ances but few close friends. Once he cites examples of his behavior, though, it becomes apparent that he was not a monster
in the conventional sense. The monster in Lem is his playful
but dogged refusal to accept any authority he considers unwor-
thy of his respect. As a child he did not act out his resistance to
authority, but from the autobiography it is evident that Lem
thoroughly disagreed with much that took place around him.
His personality as a child is best described as reflective, irrev-
erent, somewhat distant, occasionally ambivalent, deeply individualistic, and highly creative. His adult personality and his
work are very similar.

Lem's description of his adolescence includes a bit more
conventional biographical detail, as he nostalgically reflects on
several teachers and friends, but he still refers to the friends in
vague terms such as "Jurek G." or "Julek D." and notes that he
cannot recall the faces of his neighbors. The most striking feature of this period in his life is his deepening sense of distance
from people and events around him. At this point in the autobiography he mentions the "high castle," with its obvious allusions to separation from others.

Lem says that his youthful years were unremarkable, describing himself as fat and physically weak and saying that his
father did not beat him, while his mother slapped him only

once. His insistence on an unremarkable childhood notwith-standing, two features of those years stand out—his imagina-tive, quirky rendition of his thoughts and the passion with which he approached reading. For instance, he mentions wanting siblings but adds that he would only have used them as little slaves! He read voraciously—encyclopedias for entries on elephants, birds, plants, and the physiology of the Negro; anatomy and science books; and Jules Verne, H. G. Wells, Sta-pledon, Rilke, Conrad, Saint-Exupery, Fedro, Karl May, and many East European writers, including Sienkiewicz, Slwacki, and Pitigrilli. Later, he was also influenced by Dostoevsky, Gombrowicz, and Bruno Schulz. Lem's imaginative approach to intellectual or creative activity remains evident.

Of his creativity, he commented recently that he virtually never knows where he is headed as he begins a book. "This casual, improvised, spontaneous way of writing is the general characteristic of all I do. For, surprising as it may seem, it is also true with discursive [sic] books. When I started writing 'Summa . . .'—I had no plan, no clear-cut draft. In a word it was an open work. . . . I just spontaneously and organically took to writing."

Lem's interests have also remained diverse. They have spilled over into his rage to avoid repetition, so that he detests and fears repeating himself in his books. Consequently, any reader intent on pigeonholing writers by genre will have a dif-ficult time categorizing Lem's works. He has experimented with thirty genres, including poetry, short stories, novels, sci-ence fiction, detective fiction, fantasy, scientific treatises, liter-ary criticism, cybernetic theory, sociological material, book reviews of works that do not exist, book reviews of works that do exist, philosophical essays, literary critical theory, extended polemical responses to his critics, autobiography, radio plays, film scripts, television plays, and saga novels with recurrent characters.

In addition to traditional literary and scientific sources, he was also influenced by popular culture in the first film "talk-ies" where he saw Jolson, King Kong, and Boris Karloff. As an adult, he has been willing to pay attention to pop culture forms and to utilize them, but in doing so he has applied the literary standards associated with serious fiction and essay writing. His insistence on imposing quality in pop forms has contributed significantly to serious East European readers and critics accepting science fiction much earlier than their counterparts in the United States.

During Lem's adolescence, his iconoclastic resistance to incompetent authority figures developed into a barely concealed disgust that manifested itself, in his autobiography, in the form of a long harsh critique on "paper writing" in the schools and on a military camp he attended. He was not opposed to work or to writing, but he loathed being forced to write on topics that did not interest him or that were not conducive to discoveries. When forced to do an assignment, he was often sloppy in his work, showing little interest in or aptitude for detail. However, when working independently, he found himself, much to his own surprise, capable of patient, close work with experimental projects or theory. He became intrigued with water and electricity experiments, built an electric motor, and once worked on constructing a pedalless bicycle, which would somehow gallop.

When he finished his college-level work at Karol Szajnochas Gymnasium in 1939, he decided to proceed with medical studies at Lvov Medical Institute. The years between 1939 and 1950, before he took creative writing seriously, were turbulent ones for Lem, partly because of World War II, but also, in part, because he started translating some of his iconoclastic thoughts into action. His medical studies were interrupted in 1941 when the war forced the closing of all Polish universities. During the remaining war years, Lem took on various jobs, working as a welder and as a car mechanic for a German business. The situation was quite dangerous, but he has joked about it in interviews by noting that he got involved in a bit of sabotage because he was such a poor mechanic.

In 1944, when the Red Army freed Lvov and reopened the universities, Lem resumed his medical studies at Lvov. In 1946 he moved with his parents to Cracow. There he finished his

Medical Absolutorium in 1948 at Jagellonian University without having taken a diploma, because anyone with a medical diploma was being drafted for life as a military doctor, a prospect that did not excite Lem.

He had begun working in 1947 as a scientific research assistant at Jagellonian University and became involved in editing the state-financed journal *Życie Nauki*. While there, he published several scientific articles in the journal. During these years with *Życie Nauki* he first read about the topic that has become his life-long concern—cybernetics.

Lem ventured into literary writing in 1946 when he wrote and published a few poems and short stories. The poems appeared in a weekly Catholic paper, *Tygodnik Powszechny*, and the three stories in the Kattowitz weekly named *New World of Adventure*. One of those short stories was science fiction, while another was about espionage in Oak Ridge. Lem is not certain how he came to write science fiction or where his interest first developed. Shortly thereafter he published a few more short stories including "Garden of Darkness," which were "lyrical-romantic tales" and stylistic imitations of Rilke's work.

He finished his first novel, *Czas nieutracony (Time Not Lost*, untranslated), and submitted it to a private publisher in 1948 (Gebethner and Wolff), but the house folded. Then, because the manuscript was considered politically controversial for its discussion of cybernetics, it meandered through all of the state-run publishing houses until 1954–1955. It was finally published in a thoroughly rewritten version. The editorial process, which substantially altered the book, was so stringent that Lem refers to that experience as "mild brain washing." The version currently available in Polish and German is the original rendition, written prior to the "editing" process. Lem also wrote *Astronauci (Astronauts*, untranslated) around this time, a book that he describes as a "naive SF novel." The period between 1948 and 1950 was especially difficult for him because he had decided not to practice medicine but had yet to settle on a career as a writer.

In 1951 he wrote a play with Roman Hussari called *Jacht*

Paradise (*Yacht Paradise,* untranslated) that was produced by a theater group in Szcercin. Between 1952 and 1955, he also wrote scientific articles for the weekly *New Culture.*

On August 29, 1953, during the interim between the composition and the publication of *Time Not Lost,* he married Barbara Lesniak, who is a practicing physician. During the early 1950s, Lem was in a delicate situation politically as a person without a visible career. He had been expelled from the Authors League in 1951 for not having a published book to his credit, he had no medical diploma, and he had no job because he had been forced to relinquish his editorial position with *Życie Nauki.*

In 1955 he and his wife moved to Kliny, a suburb of Cracow, where they took up residence in a house they inherited. They still live in Kliny today. Lem's father died that year, a loss that continues to arouse strong emotions for Lem. As recently as 1981, he noted that his father worked at the hospital the day he died, an unusual detail to recall twenty-five years later in an interview. In 1955 he also received the first of many literary awards that would be bestowed upon him: The Golden Order of Merit from the city of Cracow.

Lem's period of mature writing began after 1956. During the dozen years between 1956 and 1968 Lem was extremely productive, writing nineteen projects. These include five science-fiction novels, ten books of science-fiction short stories that initiate his four cycles (Pirx the Pilot, Ijon Tichy, the robot fairy tales, and the Trurl-Klapaucius cycle), one science-fiction play, and three television plays. He also wrote a book on cybernetic sociology and his theoretical masterpiece—*Summa technologiae,* a 650–page treatise that has been described as "breathtakingly brilliant and risky."

During these years he published the works that garnered him a pan-European reputation as one of the strongest literary writers of the mid-twentieth century: *Star Diaries* (1957), *The Investigation* (1959), *Return from the Stars* (1961), *Solaris* (1961), *Memoirs Found in a Bathtub* (1961), *The Invincible* (1964), *Cyberiad* (1965), and *His Master's Voice* (1968). Lem's work became very popular, especially with Russian readers, so that his books have been translated into thirty languages and have sold well over eleven million copies. By the end of the twelve-year golden period, positive critical commentary was abundant. Lem was being hailed as "the Titan of East European science fiction," and as "one of the most significant SF writers of our century and a distinctive voice in world literature." His countrymen were also beginning to recognize the merit of his work, as was apparent when he won the Second Degree Literary Award from the Polish Minister of Culture and Art (1965).

When he began to write *Philosophy of Chance,* an attempt to establish an empirical theory of literature, he realized how little he knew about structural linguistics. Characteristic of Lem, he responded to this shortcoming by studying mathematical linguistics and structuralist literature for a full year.

After 1968, he seems to have encountered a crisis that prompted significant experimentation with literary form. An example is *A Perfect Vacuum,* which contains a series of satirical, zany reviews about nonexistent books. Lem has indicated dissatisfaction with some of his early theoretical writing, but most especially he developed a "resistance to science fiction creativity" out of a sense that the genre was suffering " 'ecological pollution' . . . in terms of theme and repertoire." In the intervening fourteen years, he has written a substantial number of nonfiction books (criticism, theory, cybernetics, and philosophy) in which he expresses deep concern about man's future, but he has written little new fiction. During this time, though, a number of books with new titles have recollected or rearranged previously published material. Since Lem is only in his early sixties, he may still renew his commitment to fiction writing.

As his interest in traditional science fiction has waned, Lem has become more directly involved once again in scientific matters, writing in journals such as *Philosophical Studies* and becoming a member of the Commission "Poland 2000," a division of the Polish Academy of Sciences. His reputation among scientists is such that he was the sole nonscientist invited in 1971 to the Soviet-American Conference on Extra-Terrestrial

Intelligence. In the late 1960s he began receiving literary awards quite regularly, and in 1973 he won the First Degree Award from the Minister of Culture and Art.

Lem also became involved in a continuing dialogue with other science-fiction writers and academic theoreticians—in journals such as *Quarber Merkur, Science-Fiction Studies,* and *Science Fiction Commentary.* In 1973 the Science Fiction Writers of America bestowed an honorary membership on Lem, but four years later, in 1977, writers whom he had criticized used a technicality to engineer its revocation.

Lem's high standards and his critical reaction to science fiction have been the chief source of the rancor. He considers much American science fiction windy, unoriginal re-presentations of an idea and only pseudoscientific. Ironically, Lem has been criticized for not including enough "hardware" in his science-fiction novels and for suggesting that many scientific problems have no answer. Lem has retorted that another problem with science fiction is the "pretense that insoluble problems (such as those of a logical typus) are soluble." He also feels that contemporary science fiction lacks something, although he is not certain what. He believes that the problem may stem from an insufficient theoretical base for the genre. He is waiting, he notes, for new philosophical thoughts, new sociological concepts, galactic variety, insight into the thoughts of "Automatons," insight into fate, and new thoughts on the nature of the universe.

The substance of his complaint alone would never have set off a quarrel as nasty as the Science Fiction Writers Association debacle, but the tone of some Lem comments, coming from a foreigner living in a Communist country, was more than enough to incite wrath. He wrote several highly critical articles between 1973 and 1975 in *Science-Fiction Studies* that were dominated by reasoned, if acerbic, comments about the genre. His statement that "practically all SF is trash" did not do much to win friends, but it could not be construed as a personal attack. Even a title as inflammatory as "Philip K. Dick: A Visionary Among Charlatans" did not set off an explosion.

However, an article in the *Frankfurter Allgemeine Zeitung* (February 22, 1975) was very blunt and contained disparaging references to specific authors, so that when published in the *SFWA Forum*, it evoked an incredible uproar, resulting in an international scene and the revocation of Lem's honorary membership.

The revocation move then prompted a protracted public debate (through letters in the science-fiction journals) between Lem's antagonists and his supporters, involving the most prominent figures in the American science-fiction community. The article in the *Frankfurter Allgemeine Zeitung* had been sufficiently strident to create problems, but to make matters worse, it took three years for anyone to discover and indicate in print that the American reprinter—who should not be dignified with the appellation "Translator"—had "adapted" the German newspaper article so freely that he had transformed a stringent piece of criticism into a bone-jarring, sensationalistic, almost rude diatribe. One example suffices to illustrate the incredible liberties taken. Lem's title had actually been "SF, or Phantasy Come to Grief." The reprinter rendered it in English as "Looking Down on Science Fiction: A Novelist's Choice for the World's Worst Writing." Instead of generating much-needed light in American science-fiction circles, the article in the German newspaper (as rendered in the English translation) led to a great quantity of unproductive heat.

In the meantime, Lem lectured twice at Jagellonian University. The first year he was associated with the Philology Faculty, lecturing on literature; during his second tenure, he spent two years on the Philosophy Faculty.

Lem's nonliterary affiliations and interests are as diverse as his literary forms. He is cofounder of the Polish Astronautical Society and a member of the Polish Cybernetics Association. He has continued studying cybernetics and has worked on the theory of evolution and everything at the elementary level having to do with philosophy and physics. He has been most influenced by Vienna-circle philosophers such as Russell and Wittgenstein. He reads in four foreign languages—German,

English, French and Russian—so that he can keep up with scientific literature in the original. He learned English from the
lectures of Russell, Norbert Wiener, Wittgenstein, Sir Arthur
Stanley Eddington, and Richard Feynman, whose works he
studied for the science but also for the quality of the prose.

He has noted that his favorite writer is Shakespeare (and
Hamlet his favorite character in literature), his favorite artist
Hieronymous Bosch, his favorite composer Chopin, and *Don
Quixote* his favorite book. Lem has no hobbies, but he plays
tennis and tries his hand at skiing. He also enjoys the company
of his son, Tomek, born March 14, 1968.

Lem's most recent book, *Wizja Lokalna (Official Hearing
On the Spot,* untranslated) appeared in 1982 in Poland. That
year his Polish publisher also initiated a new series of his selected works.

During 1982–83 Lem spent a year in West Berlin at the Institute for Advanced Study, writing and reading material he
missed during the year of Polish martial law.

Currently Lem is working on a Tichy novel that he has tentatively dubbed "LEM" (for "Lunar Expedition Misery"). It
depicts "autonomous robot developments." He has not done
much fiction writing lately, but he is also talking of one new
Pirx story and a new collection of reviews on books "that do
not exist but should."

Lem has been careful since the 1950s to disguise his criticism
of the Communist regime in the East, but anyone writing material as critical as his lives dangerously. His Western supporters are very concerned about his safety in Poland during the
current unrest and martial law. Despite opportunities to flee to
the West, Lem has insisted that he wishes to remain in his na-
tive Poland.

Lem's approach to life, one which drives him to explore
problems that may not yield solutions and then to insist that
writers be honest about reporting their continuing inability to
discover solutions, makes him a difficult taskmaster—for himself and for others in the literary community. That he finds
himself set apart is not surprising when he explains his percep-
tion of the function of art. He said, "[Art] gives man a remind-

er that he is not just a consumer but a creator as well. It awakens in him the urge to struggle and perform great deeds; it fills him with the craving to pass on the Promethean fire to generations to come." Lem stands apart because he is attempting to be a creator and not just a consumer.

2

Tichy at Large:

Star Diaries
and
Memoirs of a Space Traveler

Lem spent twenty years writing the stories that appear in *Dzienniki gwiazdowe* (first Polish edition 1957, fourth edition, 1971). The American edition divides the collection into separate books—*Star Diaries* (1976) and *Memoirs of a Space Traveler* (1981). The *Star Diaries* collection has twelve stories (all numbered voyages), while the second collection, containing nine stories, offers two numbered voyages, five reminiscences, an Ijon Tichy story, and Tichy's open letter to the universe. All tales in both volumes include space adventures or futuristic settings involving Ijon Tichy. The long gestation period for the collection shows. The tone varies from whimsy to heavy intellectual discussion. The stories also vary in complexity, as some are simply anecdotes, while others comprise sophisticated philosophical arguments about ontology, metaphysics, and epistemology. And the length of the stories ranges from seven to sixty-two pages so that some are one-idea tales while others are substantial novellas with numerous themes.

Star Diaries is a collection of stories, so it does not contain a continuous plot. Nevertheless, there are unifying elements. Themes recur, topics for satire overlap, the character Tichy reappears, and the setting is always in outer space.

The truly significant unifying elements, though, are not overt. The first factor that creates cohesion is the tone developed by the narrator, who always establishes substantial distance between himself and conventional social practices, as in the thirteenth voyage, when Tichy refuses to side with either of the story's antithetical forces, Pinta or Panta, which are vying for his allegiance. Lem establishes the distance through many means, the most striking of which is satire. Lem satirizes all sorts of topics, people, and institutions, but he imposes no systematized method, opting instead for repeated, random jabs at his targets. Some satiric thrusts are as brief as a paragraph. This random use of satire fosters unity because it provides the reader with a familiar generic mode.

Another significant recurrent element, the philosophical tale from the Swiftian tradition, follows from the satiric mode as Lem contemplates issues such as man's place in the universe, the role of religion, or the nature of history as a form of intellectual discourse. Invariably these tales involve making fun of or attacking the proponent of a particular intellectual position. The jest or the attack then develops into a "veritable orgy of parodies." These three devices—distancing, satire, and philosophical tale—create unity by exploring various elements of the human experience. The final cohesive element is the "consistency of theme" wherein Lem mocks man's pretensions, parodies history, and discusses time travel.

Thematically, the stories in *Memoirs* are passingly similar to those in *Star Diaries*. But Lem sharpens the thematic focus in the later volume by concentrating on an investigation of what happens when man exercises his capacity for invention without being able to anticipate adequately what will result.

Finally, the stories in *Memoirs of a Space Traveler* adhere more closely to traditional plotting practice (with an Aristotelian beginning, middle, and end) and concentrate more on "story" than on philosophical disquisition. Ideas are still present, but they do not usurp plot and character as they sometimes do in *Star Diaries*.

The plots incorporate many different topics, including, for example, time loops (seventh voyage), humanity's candidacy in the United Planets (eighth), clones (fourteenth) and a genealogy of Tichy's family (twenty-eighth). However, as Michael Kan-

del points out in his note at the end of *Star Diaries,* the plots in
this first book fall into three basic types: playful anecdote,
pointed satire, and outright philosophy.

The twenty-second voyage (1954) best illustrates the playful
anecdote. After he has begun the voyage, Ijon Tichy discovers,
to his decided disappointment, that he has lost his penknife.
Then he lands on Andrygon, a location he describes as "an old,
dilapidated wreck of a planet, which should have been taken
out of circulation long ago." He has arrived during the school's
final exams and finds himself having to prove that life on Earth
is possible (because the Andrygonians are convinced that such
a possiblity would constitute "an anomaly of nature").

The most sustained incident has Tichy listening to Father
Lacymon relate the difficulties that Father Oribazy enoun-
tered in doing missionary chores. In his zeal to teach ignorant
natives about church martyrs, Father Oribazy describes the
sacrifices of saints such as John, who allowed himself to be
boiled alive in oil. The natives are skeptical but after repeatedly checking with the good Father about his professed desire to
be a saint, they accommodate his wishes in a literal fashion that
he had not anticipated. As Father Lacymon finishes his tale
about the "problems" involved in missionary work, Tichy,
much to his delight, locates the lost penknife, an insignificant
event that contrasts with the weightier circumstances of the
story, all the more because of Tichy's reaction. Lem's denouement involves a grotesque sequence, yet the anecdote is humorous, because Lem is playing with what would happen if
various exaggerations were taken seriously. The device of the
lost penknife adds whimsy.

While some other Lem tales are as light as this one, most are
more astringent. The twenty-fifth voyage (1954) illustrates the
second type of tale: pointed satire. In this case, the satire is di-
rected at methods of scientific research and at people who engage in factionalism in philosophy and theology. The subject in
this case is the application of scientific methods in the great
potato hunt. The precipitating event occurs when a "brave
hunter" is attacked by the deadly potato (that is, a "multicel-
lular organism well known on Earth, namely the *Solanum*

tuberosum, a bulbaceous, gametopetalous, multiseminiferous species." Lem's use of ironic deflation quickly sets the tone for the remainder of the tale. "It is difficult to describe what took place after . . . it turned out that Gorbras had brought back on his spacesuit bits of potato leaves. The intrepid stellar adventurer, stung to the quick by the insinuation that for four straight hours he had been fighting potatoes, demanded an immediate retraction of this vile calumny." As Lem describes reactions by the contending scientific factions, including the physicalists, the semanticists, and the neopositivists, the spoof becomes increasingly ridiculous, until finally a faction develops that is called the "holists-pluralists-behaviorists-physicalists."

The third plot type, Lem's philosophical tales, divides into two modes, the playful and the serious. *The twentieth voyage* (1971) illustrates the playful mode. In this novella-length story, set in the twenty-seventh century, Ijon Tichy gets a visit from himself, Ijon Tichy, asking him, Ijon Tichy, to direct an organization called THEOHIPPIP (that is, Teleotelechronistic-Historical Engineering to Optimize the Hyputerized Implementation of Paleological Programming and Interplanetary Planning). Were Tichy a man who sought power or were he an evil person, this satire would not carry the same force. As is, Tichy is a personable, bumbling, well-intentioned guy who makes an incredible mess of history, especially when he assumes a measure of power like God or Zeus in Greek mythology. Because Tichy is depicted as a fallible person, the reader does not become distracted by his concern with Tichy's motives or with ideological issues. Instead, the reader concentrates on the insidious problems that arise when man pretends to be capable of more than he really is able to handle. Lem is convincing because Tichy's persona takes over to explain various anomalies in nature, and the detail persuades us that Tichy's is a real, even if bizarre, world.

As Tichy reconstructs history, his project passes through three phases—Genesis (given over to scientists), Historical Division (to philosophers and artists), and Social Affairs. During the second phase, the most interesting of the three, Lem uses the roman à clef device to achieve his imaginative zenith.

Here Tichy explains how he handles a group he labels "unprincipled designers," whom he must fire from their jobs and pack off to other historical eras. Homer Gumby ends up in ancient Greece, where he writes books. "*The Iliad* and *Odyssey* are *roman à clef;* the irascible Zeus, for instance, that's a satire on me [Tichy]."

One of the most telling philosophical scenes arises when Tichy explains the history of evolution and man's relation to it. His assistant Goody designs a project named BARF (Binary Anthropogenesis for Reciprocal Feedback). Tichy gets a bit concerned about his assistant when Goody gives dolphins "frontal radar." Alarmed, Tichy forces his assistant to curtail the project at this point. He then accepts the monkey as "a working model for the program." This fiasco leads to the creation of God who offers the " 'discreet assistance' " that comes to be known as miracles. Ultimately, though, Tichy learns a painful lesson about the revision of history: "Every telechronic intervention set off an avalanche of events, which couldn't be held in check without appropriate measures, and those in turn produced new perturbations." Poor Tichy finds that when man oversteps his limits, he wreaks havoc with his own environment. Since the twentieth voyage is devoted almost exclusively to parodistic detail concerning two philosophical issues—the nature of history and man's relation to it—the tale is literary but its subject is philosophical.

The twenty-first voyage (1971) illustrates Lem's serious philosphical mode. This 62–page novella is quite unlike the twentieth voyage because it utilizes virtually no individualized characters. Instead, Lem works with prototypes, schools of thought, or intellectual positions as a pretext to pursue and satirize philosophical arguments in an undisguised fashion. Many passages, taken out of context, could easily be passed off as pure philosophy.

In the narrative frame for this story, Lem dispatches Tichy to Dichotica where he meets Father Darg, proponent of a new faith called Duism. The story consists of a history of Duism and debate among Tichy, Darg, and a few other shadowy, undeveloped figures over issues such as the immortalization of man, physiological engineering, faith, God, freedom, orthodoxy, and mind control.

The sections on physical aberrations and "autoevolutionary" physical development do not succeed especially well as literature, but once Lem begins his discussion of God and faith, the twenty-first voyage becomes a fascinating, albeit disturbing, essay on man's approach to faith and freedom in an age of cynicism. The chief problem under discussion is how the individual relates to government and society. The Dichoticans' faith—Duism—is ultimately a paradox: "You believe by doubting and you doubt by believing; yet this state too is not the final one." The compelling, unsettling complication is that this group is willing to proselytize by using machines to control minds; hence, no need for missionary work by humans. The ultimate paradox arises when the Prior indicates that his society's unlimited capacity for mastery of its environment—a virtual omnipotence—leaves people with no need or desire to act. "Nothing remains for us then but to sit here among the fossils of rats, in this maze of 'dried-up sewers'." When Tichy leaves, he is a changed man. This difficult, often slow-moving tale represents Lem in one of his darker moods.

Nearly all of the stories collected in the second portion of the *Star Diaries* (that is, in *Memoirs Of a Space Traveler*) present unappreciated inventors and scientists each of whom has a single obsession. In the collection's eighteenth journey we again find Tichy acting as God, but this time he has vountarily chosen the role. In the "Further Reminiscences" section, Tichy is visited by or seeks out a series of strange scientists. In Reminiscence I (1961), Corcoran has invented a "world"; in IV (1961), Molteris has developed a time machine; in V (1963), Newton and Snodgrass initiate an escalating campaign to improve washing machines; and in "Doctor Diagoras" (1964), Diagoras works on an invention for which he has no plan.

Each of these invention stories begins with a typical science-fiction device, but then Lem includes a twist that incorporates a fresh perspective on the time-worn device. For example, once Tichy is in the lab of a scientist named Zazul, he sees a pair of trousered legs in an alcohol solution and threatens to re-

port the scientist to the authorities for having killed a man in
order to set up a cloning operation. Zazul bets him that when
he learns the detail behind the specimen Tichy will not report
him. The problem, it turns out, is that Zazul cloned himself
and then, when he decided he wanted a permanent record of
his achievement, got into a disagreement with the clone over
who should be "preserved" in alcohol. Unfortunately for this
"constructor," the clone was the victor in the ensuing struggle
for control. As the story ends, Tichy concedes to Zazul, the
clone, that he has won the bet. Tichy cannot report a clone for
murdering its creator. Through humorous twists, in this and
other stories, Lem reinforces the dominant theme in *Memoirs:*
artificial intelligence will develop independently of man once
it evolves sufficiently.

A striking feature of *Star Diaries* and *Memoirs* is Lem's inventiveness in four areas—wordplay, names, humor, and incidents in the plot. The quality of his wordplay and his choice of
names is most evident in the twentieth voyage, where Tichy is
Director of THEOHIPPIP. Examples of choice acronyms include GENESIS (which stands for Generators for the Establishment of Isochronalities), CUPID (Cyclochronic Unidirectional
Polarization of Inchoate Differentials), and BIPPETY (for Bio-
genetic Implementation of Parameters to Perfect Terrestrial
Intelligence). Interesting names among errant program direc-
tors in Tichy's project to revise history include, in addition to
Homer Gumby, P. Lado (Plato), Harris Doddle (Aristotle),
Lenny D.Vinch (Leonardo da Vinci), and Harry Bosch (Hieronymous Bosch).

With respect to humor, Lem's imagination emerges primarily through understatement, as in the twenty-third voyage
(1961), which is about a group of "Whds" who have virtually
perfected the miniaturization process. Tichy notes that "certain risks" are involved in this readily available miniaturization
process, but this is a mild understatement. Two incidents illustrate Lem's humor. Once Tichy spills a gray powder on the
floor only to have a Whdian exclaim: "Look out, you're spilling
my daddy." For daddy, the risk in miniaturization is indeed
grave. Another time, Tichy nearly self-destructs when he be-

comes unduly enthusiastic and the miniaturization device jams, reconstructing him as "Napoleon Bonaparte in imperial uniform."

This incessant, inventive use of humorous understatement becomes an important aspect of the persona for Tichy and many other Lem characters because it reflects their paradoxical position. They are forever attempting something grandiose, only to see the project backfire. Eventually, an interesting temperament arises: the character is open to new possiblities, but he is still reticent in a fashion that wins the reader's heart. Lem's humor reinfores this aspect of his character's persona.

Lem's inventiveness with respect to plot is especially evident in the stories from *Memoirs*. For example, in "Reminiscence II" (1961), Decantor announces that he has spent forty-eight years inventing an immortal human soul, but Tichy tells him that people will not want the static immortality that Decantor describes, so most likely no one will buy his product. Having killed his wife and invested forty-eight of his fifty-eight years in order to produce this soul, Decantor is disappointed that no one will be interested. Tichy, though, is horrified by what Decantor has done, so instead of investing money in the project, as Decantor has requested, Tichy buys the soul and smashes it. Then he announces that he has killed the immortal soul.

Because of Lem's fertile imagination, he adds a dimension to his plots that few writers ever achieve. The zany quality reflects an attitude that Dominique Sila, a Lem critic, says is an essential element of Lem's outlook on life. Lem has rejected traditional values and structures and is utilizing his rich imagination to cope with the problem of needing new values and to create a new world. In the process, Lem encounters the awesome nothingness of the universe and subsequent existential absurdity. The absurdity is sufficiently disconcerting that a playful attitude aids in defusing man's terror. In this absurd situation, man will distinguish himself only if he creates something new; hence, Lem's obsession with inventors and constructors.

Science fiction, then, is also the most appropriate genre for

Lem, because it allows him to search more openly for his new world. Sila notes, though, that the best source for rich inventiveness is in a child's playful approach to life. Thus, the powerful infusion of whimsical imagination into most of Lem's work, not just *Star Diaries*, contributes significantly to his sense of how man can survive in the threatening conditions of the late twentieth century.

In *Star Diaries* he touches on many of the themes that will occupy him for the next twenty years. The most important of these is man's situation in the universe. Lem is concerned with what makes man unique and with the tools he needs to survive in an alien, hostile environment. Essential to survival, Lem asserts, is each individual's creative, untrammeled exercise of the imagination. Here he alludes to man's Godlike status in the universe, and at times he seems to revel in the power and the brilliance of man's ingeniousness. He is willing to concede the wonder of many technological advances.

Invariably, though, Lem pulls the reader up short by calling attention to the folly in man's attempt to be God; this point is rendered in a particularly delightful manner in the eighteenth and twentieth voyages. When he portrays man's folly, he utilizes humor, irony, and playfulness, and he depicts man in a variety of guises, including, most conspicuously, the bumbler (in the eighteenth, twentieth, and twenty-third voyages, and in "Reminiscence IV"). In this guise, man is unable to foresee adequately the consequences of his actions. Tichy almost always accepts responsibility for his faulty efforts and pleads good intentions, thereby defusing a reader's anger about his costly errors.

In Star Diaries Lem approaches the first of many paradoxes that will appear in his work: man is capable of wondrous creations but only rarely does he develop his inventions without prompting many thorny problems. For Lem, man has boundless potential to do good but delivers very little. This paradox is existential, and it prompts Lem to formulate a description of man uncannily similar to Camus's in *The Myth of Sisyphus*. Tichy makes the point in "Reminiscence I" when he says of his strange guest inventors that each has a single obsession causing him to "burn with that consuming fire of objectivity that forces a man to renew efforts that are doomed to failure." Man ennobles himself through his effort, but he is nevertheless not going to succeed.

The paradox takes an inverse form in the twenty-first voyage: if man were omnipotent (capable of doing anything he pleased), he would have no motivation to do anything. This paradox from Duism (phrased as "because we can, we do not") leads to a belief in an obvious contradiction: the existence of an impenetrable and mysterious God who is in many respects tantalizingly similar to man. Thus, the Duistic paradox may be approached as the dark side of man's condition with respect to potential and action.

Lem also notes that man incessantly but futilely attempts to plan his creativity or at least to know in advance what he will create when he explores. This thematic point is very nicely rendered in "Reminiscence I" and in "Doctor Diagoras." Much to Tichy's delight, Corcoran manages to create a world in a box that is an exact replica of the real one—no mean accomplishment. Nevertheless, Doctor Diagoras disparages Corcoran's feat by indicating that it is merely mimicry. He, Doctor Diagoras, is working on a truly significant possibility—development of fungoids—in which he does not know what he seeks. Lem seems to agree with Diagoras that charting unexplored territory is more noteworthy than planned research. Ironically, in this story, though, Lem conveniently fails to note that spontaneous quests such as Diagoras's are often the source of the follies for which he so regularly chastises man, as when Tichy bungles the reverse acceleration of an electron (eighteenth voyage).

In a nascent form, Lem raises a final thematic point about man's state, which he will develop more fully in *Solaris* and *The Invincible*. This is man's desperate need to maintain communication with other men and alien forces. The idea surfaces in "Reminiscence II" when Decantor indicates that his manufactured soul will be blind, deaf, and paralyzed for eternity (i.e., not able to communicate in any fashion). Tichy is revolted and horrified at the prospect of no change and of total silence. Yet this thematic thrust is redolent with implicit irony because later in his career Lem will scathingly attack man for striving so desperately to establish contact with alien forces or phenomena.

A second, implicit thematic issue follows from Lem's attitude toward man and more particularly toward man's creativity. Lem despises any social force that resorts to tyranny, induces conformity, or calls for perfection. He is probably so vehement about these issues because they threaten man's freedom; more importantly, though, they jeopardize the exercise of creativity. Lem does not develop this theme through expository speeches. It shows up in his biting satiric attacks on the institutions that foster tyranny, conformity, and the illusion of perfection (especially in the twelfth and twenty-fourth voyages).

This concern with tyranny may explain Lem's curious, unpredictable attitude toward Western and Communist political institutions that often puzzles readers. In the twenty-fourth voyage (1961), he begins with a spoof on "Civic Initiative" (i.e., free enterprise). By the time the tale closes, though, it is not nearly so clear that the capitalistic West is the sole object of his derision. After his initial escapade with the authorities (the *Życie Nauki* incident and the censorship of *Time Not Lost*), Lem most likely remained politically "safe" in a precarious political situation in Poland because he so often sets his satiric material in the West. This may be a deliberate ploy on Lem's part (even if not intentional, it is effective), but the Eastern bloc does not escape the *Star Diaries* cycle of stories unscathed. Lem's approach to tyranny would seem to indicate that he is neither pro-West nor pro-East, because in their desire for monolithic control, both superpowers threaten to shackle the opportunities for an artist or thinker to exploit his creativity to its fullest extent.

The final significant thematic development concerns man's relation to the artificial intelligence he creates, such as robots. Lem initiates his discussion in three tales when he talks about man as creator (or God). At this point he does not offer much detail on his views, but he relates the theme from a different perspective in each tale. In "Reminiscence I," when, almost as an afterthought, Corcoran assesses his ability to invent a world in a box, he questions whether we are boxes on shelves, too, for some higher God, who exists, in his turn, within the box of a God who exists on yet another, even higher plane. The tone here is one of wonderment and curiosity. In "Reminiscence V," the creations get out of hand and lead to a hilarious yet bizarre, almost Kafkaesque denouement. In this case, the humor dominates, black though it is.

In "Doctor Diagoras," Lem evokes *Frankenstein* as the tale closes, but without the high camp tone of "Reminiscence V." The spooky monster in Lem's story threatens to run amok, but Lem depicts Doctor Diagoras in a realistic fashion and bestows a serious high-mindedness on his character that distinguishes this story from *Frankenstein.* Here Diagoras is asserting the nobility of man's capacity to create new knowledge and to foster spontaneity in his creations, so that the dominant tone is almost triumphant. The eerie, frightening element is significant because of its placement in the story's denouement, but it has nowhere near the force of the preceeding optimism.

In *Star Diaries,* Lem approaches his theme about artificial intelligence (cybernetics) indirectly through plot incident and tone. Subsequently in *Cyberiad* he will be much more direct and thorough in examining the philosophical and sociological ramifications.

Lem's approach to theme is fairly traditional, but in his characterization technique he usually defies Aristotelian standards in one major respect. He develops one or two characters intensely and then peoples the story with a gallery of stereotypes, caricatures, mouthpieces for philosophical positions, and shadowy phantoms who serve only to facilitate the movement and development of the protagonist and one or two other characters at most. Lem's technique is not bred of an inability to flesh out characters but of his sense that most individuals "see" the world in the fashion he employs in his characterization technique. In *Star Diaries* the only character who is thoroughly fleshed out is Ijon Tichy. A few characters such as Father Darg in the twenty-first voyage emerge from shadow-

dom, but most do not. In *Memoirs* the eccentric scientists in
the "Reminiscence" sections become credible foils for Tichy,
but even these characters have more in common with a stereotype of the brilliant, weird scientist than they do with fully-de-
veloped central characters. Tichy is as well-developed here as
any character, but he acts more as implied author, facilitating
Lem's own views, than he does as an active character in a literary work.

The character of Tichy assumes numerous "shapes" from
story to story so that finally the question arises: who is Tichy?
Tom Lewis provides a solid starting point when he writes that
"Tichy himself is a paradox, a man of the most ordinary sensi-
bilities and petty concerns concealed beneath a cloak of
intellectual prowess, personal ambition, and renowned accomplishments. For although he has acquired a reputation as the
most resourceful and enterprising space voyager of his age, he
is nevertheless easily intimidated, often the butt of ridicule,
prone to carelessness, and given to let things slide." Paradox is
the key word in Lewis's depiction of Tichy, because the character does shift wildly, albeit plausibly, between alleged brilliance and gross ineptitude. Sometimes he is the sage who
listens with forbearance while fools prattle on; at other times,
though, he is the foolish inventor or the bumbling space voyager. At one moment he is offensively supercilious and then later
winsomely humble. He is a conscientious man who frequently
errs, and in the process makes a mess of a situation.

Ultimately, the word *schlemiel* must be used to describe
Tichy, but he is a schlemiel with a twist. Traditionally, the
schlemiel is a likeable, well-intentioned character who never
quite succeeds; he persists good naturedly in his quest to fulfill
his goal. Eventually he wins reader sympathy for his noble if
failed tenacity in the face of overwhelming misfortune, as in
the seventh voyage when the earnest Tichy, trying to cope
with time loops, is repeatedly beaned with a hammer held by
another, future version of himself.

The twist in Tichy as schlemiel emerges when he displays
the flashes of brilliance, when he is indeed taken seriously as
an authority, and when his supercilious condescension toward

fools renders him anything but the likeable bumbler. This twist in Tichy's character does not supersede the core of his personality, but it modifies it: Tichy is the elitist's schlemiel.

In *Star Diaries*, symbolism is not a major device. For the most part, Lem's symbolism in this work acts as a reflector or as catalyst for action. In the seventh voyage the existence of only one spacesuit, for example, reflects Tichy's problem with time loops. Even though only one Tichy personality exists (and consequently only one spacesuit), there are at least two temporal manifestations of him at any given moment in the story. Thus, when both of these manifestations want a spacesuit, it becomes apparent that the story's crucial issue is time loops. In voyages twenty-two and twenty-five, the lost penknife and flashlight symbolize the triviality of events that often mar the operation of sophisticated machinery or that trigger foolishness on man's part. Likewise, the tangled underbrush through which Tichy must muddle to reach Doctor Diagoras's laboratory reflects the inchoate, unplanned nature of the scientist's research on fungoids.

On the other hand, the inventors and their inventions in *Memoirs of a Space Traveler* act as catalytic symbols (as objects that precipitate significant action in the plot). These two symbols are especially important because they indicate Lem's belief in man's unique creativity; at the same time, the inventions also indicate man's foolishness or ineptitude.

Most of this symbolism is simple in that Lem establishes one basic point and then drops the symbol. In other books, his symbolism will become more complex and more pervasive. With *Star Diaries* he seems intent on satiric attack and straight philosophical discourse rather than traditional literary matters. In fact, the overtly philosophical tales contain so little literary action that virtually no occasion for symbolism arises. In the anecdotal tales and in the "Reminiscence" stories in *Memoirs* he simply chose not to introduce much symbolism. Symbolism in the *Star Diaries* series is, then, functional but only occasionally significant.

Lem begins with simple anecdotes and gradually shifts his tone so that the philosophical elements in his work and the more complex forms dominate, but no inexorable progression exists. He mixes simple anecdote and pointed satire throughout the collection until he shifts at the end to the philosophical material.

The most telling shift in the sequence occurs in Lem's attitude. Early in his career, he balanced optimism with sober acknowledgment of problems in man's situation. He also combined tolerance for man's foibles with a sense of whimsy. Later, though, his vision became increasingly pessimistic, as is evident in a statement he made in another context: "I . . . started with a tone of 'happy futuristic optimism' and gradually arrived at a darker vision of things. . . . My pessimism (which, by the way, is far from absolute) originated with my despair in the lack of perfection to be found in human nature. . . . I was attempting in my successive books to show the inevitable handicap of the human condition."

This darker vision is apparent primarily in the tone, which has become a bit shrill and less tolerant in a sense it never was in the early tales. Lem is still capable of light moments, but they are offset significantly by the sharpness and the brooding of the philosophical tales.

Diverse as the collection is, *Star Diaries* offers an interesting overview on Lem's career because it covers his development from guarded optimism into his darker vision, as no other single title in his corpus does.

3

A Mystery of the Insoluble Typus:

The Investigation

In *Sledztwo* (*The Investigation;* 1959, 1974), Lem explores a genre other than science fiction. The main character, Lieutenant Gregory, is a Scotland Yard detective investigating a bizarre case in which corpses are moving or are being stolen from mortuaries for unknown reasons. Given all of the detective-story trappings, the reader expects that Gregory will eventually solve the case. The detective attempts to use all of the normal means to produce an explanation for the mysterious activity, relying on the search for empirical evidence. He even resorts to considering theories propounded by the brilliant, if odd, Doctor Sciss, a mathematician who argues that there has to be a statistical explanation for the phenomenon.

Toward the story's close, though, Gregory reluctantly draws the conclusion that no solution exists. His supervisor, Inspector Sheppard, upset by Gregory's willingness to acquiesce before an isolated but significant failure in the scientific method, insists on closing the case by manufacturing a plausible but false solution. Gregory, originally an advocate of scientific police work, complies with Sheppard's order to close the case, but not before vehemently indicating his disagreement with Sheppard's decision.

This novel may be read as an unusual detective story that may variously intrigue, frustrate, or even irritate the detective-fiction aficionado. But if we read the book solely on this level, a

natural question arises: why did Lem deliberately construct a
detective novel, only to undermine the most basic conventions
of the genre? The answer to the question lies in reading it as an
innovative, indirect approach to intellectual issues that he
raises throughout his career. His objective, then, is not to write
detective fiction but to utilize the genre as a vehicle for presenting his metaphysical speculation about man and truth.
Read in this way, the novel concerns the clash between traditional and contemporary values.

Throughout a large portion of the book, Gregory, as the naive detective, represents the traditional values. However, after
his startling experience with this seemingly insoluble case, the
seasoned Gregory has reluctantly concluded that if he is to be
practical and honest with himself, he must support contemporary values. And the questions facing Gregory illustrate the difference between the traditional and contemporary values. Is
truth in an absolute form accessible? What is the potential for
discovering solutions to our inevitable dilemmas? What is
man's potential in the scheme of things? Does order exist in
the universe?

Lem does not state these questions directly in the text, but
as Gregory's character evolves from dedicated detective to un-
committed skeptic, Lem is clearly grappling with these four issues. By introducing an innovative literary maneuver, he
dramatizes the clash between traditional and contemporary
values and forces the reader to experience the difference. This
device is especially effective because instead of discussing the
conflict in discursive terms, he demonstrates it by manipulating the reader's expectations.

The distinction between traditional and contemporary value systems in literature is readily apparent in the debate over
the first of the four questions. Traditional writers assume that
truth is accessible and that when it appears it is absolute, a conviction that was dominant in nineteenth-century European literature until precursors of twentieth-century developments
such as Dostoevsky and Nietzsche began questioning traditional assumptions. Recent writers have argued, to the contrary,
that if truth exists, it is obscure, fragmentary, and relative.

Contemporary novelists, especially the Europeans, offer little assurance that the protagonist will discover absolute truths. Alain Robbe-Grillet notes, for example, that the truths or the "significances of the world around us are no more than partial, provisional, even contradictory, and always contested." We might conclude, then, that detective fiction seeks out certainties within the realm of truth, while the contemporary novel searches for possibilities within the same realm.

In *The Investigation* Lem approaches the problem of truth by setting up all of the trappings of the detective novel, including Scotland Yard detectives. Even the tone of the novel—an obsessive concern with solving the case through normal police routine—derives from detective-fiction conventions. Lieutenant Gregory doggedly refuses to concede, until the very end of the book, that the phenomenon is a miracle, so even when the attempt makes him look like a fool, he badgers Sciss as his only remaining logical suspect, because he is so thoroughly convinced that an absolute, "unrelative" version of the truth exists.

After having convinced the reader that he is involved with detective fiction, Lem then introduces hints that this may not be an ordinary detective story. He refers to an invisible spirit, he describes the commission of the crime as " 'absolutely inhuman'," and he alludes to ghosts and flying saucers—all elements that point to supernatural influences.

This undermines detective-fiction conventions, because Lem describes occurrences that appear to violate natural law. The strange event treated in *The Investigation* questions our assumptions about the laws of nature, so that after we have read about corpses moving we perceive those laws in a different light, from an unfamiliar perspective. Doctor Sciss and Lieutenant Gregory offer varying hypotheses to explain what is occurring, but Lem is interested primarily in exploring the limits of our knowledge, especially with regard to science, a discipline in which we assume that our empirical data are reliable.

However, during a major portion of the novel, Doctor Sciss and Gregory attempt to use empirical data as the means to discovering a viable hypothesis for why the bodies are moving, but eventually, though, Lem's questions about the nature of

truth assume more importance than the scientific method, especially when it fails to produce the desired results. At the conclusion, a startling point has emerged clearly: Lem considers
the scientific method to be an inadequate means for ascertaining the truth. He thereby strikes out at one of the most basic
assumptions in detective fiction.

The second basic issue, the existence of solutions to our inevitable dilemmas, is closely related to the question about the
accessiblity of truth. Traditionalists are convinced that such solutions exist and that a comprehensive perspective and a complete, unified body of information is available, a position that
reflects a basic optimism. Contemporary theorists, on the other hand, contend that we work from an incomplete frame of
reference (a fragmentary perspective) and with inadequate information, a position fraught with pessimistic attitudes.

Differences in perspective on this issue, based on genre, appear immediately. The code surrounding the solution in detective novels is rigid. Not only must there be a solution, but the
criminal must be a reasonable suspect, so that the perceptive
reader has a fair opportunity to discover the solution in advance for himself.

Contemporary fiction takes a position that is almost diamet-
rically opposed. It delights in provoking the reader, even at
the close of the book, by not disclosing a solution.

As Lem approaches the issue of solutions, he is aware of divergent genre expectations, but he deliberately defies those of
detective fiction after he establishes this genre in the novel. In
his book *Summa technologiae,* Lem makes the following obser-
vation concerning solutions: "I believe in no final solutions." In
The Investigation Lem prepares the reader for the ending to a
certain extent, but the conclusion must, nevertheless, come as
a shock. One of Lem's most explicit hints that he may violate
detective-fiction conventions occurs when he describes the
strange features of this case in terms of how difficult it is to obtain a solution: "Gregory began to feel that he was standing on
the boundary between the definite and the indefinite. Each of
his thoughts seemed about to reveal one of many possible
meanings, then vanished, melting away with every desperate

effort he made to grasp it fully. And he, pursuing understanding, seemed about to plunge into a sea of ambiguous details in which he would drown, comprehending nothing even at the end."

The reader who has studied other Lem novels recognizes this passage as a foreshadowing device, but, given the dominance of detective-fiction trappings, Lem's refusal to answer the three staple questions—who, why, and how—startles the reader. Inspector Sheppard may manufacture an artificial solution for the case, which he acknowledges as false, and close the case despite Gregory's objections, but this compromise fails to ameliorate the reader's sense of shock and outrage.

The source of the reader's shock may be traced to the development of conventions concerning the ending of a novel. In traditional literature, the author provides a solution that ordinarily contributes to a closed ending (a convention upheld by the detective-fiction genre). However, since many twentieth-century writers began making extensive use of the open ending, the reader has become somewhat inured to the device; consequently, readers in general have lost the sharp sense that conventions deriving from genre considerations have evolved radically within a remarkably brief period of time.

A glance forward in Lem's corpus to *Memoirs Found in a Bathtub* corroborates this point. The protagonist and narrator, who has no name, becomes embroiled in a seemingly endless tangle of bureaucratic nonsense within the Pentagon, circa 3146, as he tries to resolve his own case (he has been informed that he has a mission but cannot determine what the mission is or how to accomplish it). The combination of existential dilemmas and science fiction/futuristic trappings so thoroughly prepares the reader for the open ending that he is not the least surprised when he fails to learn the narrator's mission and when the narrator fails to resolve his dilemma. In *The Investigation*, though, when Lem causes the reader to expect a closed ending, which would reflect detective fiction conventions, but instead provides an open ending, he vividly reminds the reader of the dramatic evolution in our values and in the literary forms that reflect those values.

The third question, concerning man's place in the scheme

of things, is a logical extension of the first two questions. Instead of asking whether truth is accessible or whether solutions exist, we now focus on man's capacity to discover the solutions that may or may not exist. The traditionalist's optimism that solutions are possible is reflected in his assumption that man is capable of bringing about those solutions. Consequently, the traditionalist's description of man's place in the universe invests him with powers that liken him to God. The contemporary writer, not nearly so sanguine about the potential for solutions, also lowers his estimation of man's capacity and, in his description, concedes man's limitations. Man is of no less interest to the twentieth-century writer than he was previously, but the estimation of his abilities has been diminished.

Detective fiction mirrors traditional assessments of man's abilities by concentrating the novel's action on a human (the detective) who is wily, highly intelligent, and endowed with unlimited skill in resolving difficult cases. Such literature exhibits confidence in man's ability to cope with his problems. Contemporary fiction, though, has thoroughly reassessed man and has found him to be sadly deficient. The most salient example of this new literary perspective on man is the rise of the antihero, who is isolated, unheroic, and unable to master his personal life or milieu.

In his approach to the third issue—man's place in the scheme of things—Lem again contravenes detective-fiction conventions, as he causes his protagonist, Gregory, to evolve from the standard detective-fiction hero into an antihero or a marginal man who ultimately rejects traditional values. Because of his experience, Gregory himself also changes his mind about what man is capable of accomplishing. As a detective, he depends upon his assumption that a criminal perpetrator exists, so initially it does not even occur to him that such an individual may not be present. When events begin to force him to consider the possiblity that inexplicable forces may be at work, he becomes apprehensive and pursues the hapless Doctor Sciss unmercifully. According to the Sherlock Holmes prototype, the detective should be master of events and should be capable of imposing order on his universe. By the end of *The In-*

vestigation, though, Lem depicts the detective as an undistinguished, limited person who is unable to master his universe, and who struggles for answers that seem not to exist. Gregory is not happy with his plight, but when the Inspector insists that they bolster traditional values by providing a semblance of order (close the case even if they have been unable to discover a solution), Gregory resists the defensive sham.

Lem conveys Gregory's dilemma explicitly when the Lieutenant explains why he has pursued Doctor Sciss so obsessively: "Actually, I'm more on the defensive, and my position is quite hopeless. I feel like a cornered rat. I only want to defend myself against the allegedly miraculous character of this case. . . . If we take this story seriously even for one moment, the ground opens up beneath our feet, our whole civilization turns into jelly, people can appear and disappear, everything is possible."

Frightening as the prospect is to him, Gregory finally accepts the possibility that there is no solution to the case and adopts a conception of man that is not nearly so grandiose as that associated with traditional values.

Had Lem portrayed Gregory as a doubter from the beginning, the surprise would not have been nearly so great, but once more Lem manipulates genre-derived expectations: he allows the reader to assume that Gregory is a traditional detective-fiction hero and then forces the reader, along with Gregory, to experience growing doubts as the protagonist adopts a twentieth-century, existential conception of man's capacity—and limitations.

If man is no longer to be depicted as master of his universe, we naturally begin asking the fourth question—about whether the order that we previously perceived in cosmic occurrences truly exists and about what forces control the universe if man does not. Traditionalists argue that universal order exists, despite man's occasional doubt or shortsightedness in perceiving it. According to contemporary values, on the other hand, such order may not exist at all, except perhaps as an artificial construction of man's mind. Moreover, alien, supernatural, or powerful natural forces may affect events and even supersede man's limited efforts.

Literary conventions concerning this fourth question—about order and power—follow logically from the answer to the second question, regarding solutions. In detective fiction, order may be disrupted during the course of the novel, but it must be restored at the conclusion and man's supremacy in the universe reasserted. In contemporary fiction, it is not uncommon, though, for an author to disrupt the world and then conclude his book without having restored order.

In his consideration of the fourth issue, Lem does not make an immediate frontal assault on traditional values. Instead, he allows the unfolding mystery involving the apparent violation of natural and biological laws to force questions: corpses simply do not come back to life and move, especially after rigor mortis has set in, so how are the characters to explain the strange events when all of the normal, scientific procedures have failed? When Lem focuses the action of the novel on a violation of biological law, he implicitly suggests that universal order has been disrupted and may not even exist. Gregory attempts to discern order by gathering empirical evidence through conventional procedures, while Doctor Sciss utilizes statistical methods to generate hypotheses and possible explanations. Gregory's deep conviction—that universal order exists—causes him to exclude religious and supernatural explanations.

When it finally becomes apparent that the scientific method is not going to yield a conventional answer, the characters, finding it difficult to accept an obvious conclusion, resort to doubtful alternatives. Sciss tenders the first of such alternatives and raises the problem of universal order when he suggests that perhaps the corpses are moving because a mutation of the cancer virus is trying "to create a new kind of order—a kind of posthumous order."

Gregory discards this hypothesis, but the suggestion is important for Lem's purposes. Traditional scientists such as Sciss would rather create doubtful hypotheses to explain a seemingly chaotic phenomenon than concede that universal order does not exist. Lem attributes such suggestions to the peculiar Doctor Sciss, whose views Gregory does not take seriously in the long run, because Lem wants the reader to realize that the attempt to deny the existence of aberrant events in nature or to rationalize them serves little purpose. A similar far-fetched reaction arises when Gregory pursues Sciss as a suspect long after it is clear that Sciss is not involved. Lem would prefer that man accommodate his description of the world, as Gregory eventually does, to include the following concession: certain events suggest that universal order may not exist (the tenuous quality of the formulation is crucial, for Lem is not arguing an absence of such order).

By having characterized Gregory as a staunch supporter of natural order who desperately desires a solution to the case, Lem renders the detective's gradually dawning, fumbling speculation about order effective in the dramatic sense; as a corollary, Gregory's conversion to contemporary values is also plausible. After his conversion, Gregory tentatively voices his concern in the following statement:

> What if everything that exists is fragmentary, incomplete, aborted, events with ends but no beginnings ... with us constantly making categories, seeking out, and reconstructing, until we think we can see total love, betrayal and defeat, although in reality we are all no more than haphazard fractions. . . . The mind, for its own self-preservation, finds and integrates scattered fragments. Using religion and philosophy as the cement, we perpetually collect and assemble all the garbage comprised by statistics in order to make sense out of things, to make everything respond in one unified voice like a bell chiming to our glory. But it's only soup. . . . [Lem's ellipses]. The mathematical order of the universe is our answer to the pyramids of chaos.

This passage sets the tone for the novel's conclusion. Lem has not asserted that chaos rules, but he has confounded both scientist and detective—symbolically the most dedicated believers in natural order—to the point where the latter is pondering whether universal order is an intellectual creation of man's mind. Thus, the bewildered reader finds the quintessen-

tial advocate of order and pattern suggesting metaphysical
heresy. The tone at the conclusion is not assertively defiant,
but it is ambivalent and provocative.

No one device in *The Investigation* is unique or even especially innovative when considered outside the context of this
novel, but the juxtaposition of the two value systems and the
peculiar violation of genre conventions provide a distinctive
literary experience. When Lem makes it clear that he will not
solve the case and that he intends to mix elements of detective
fiction and the contemporary novel so thoroughly as to with-
hold a solution, the reader finds it necessary to reevaluate his
previous impressions of the book and ask whether it succeeds
on its own terms.

Lem's mixture of conventions, far from being a flaw, is especially effective because instead of including lengthy discussion
about the debate over traditional and contemporary values, he
manipulates the reader's implicit expectations with regard to
genre to force him to experience the debate for himself in the
literary mode. Lem's response to criticism of Philip Dick's
Ubik not only provides an answer to Dick's critics but also offers a telling answer to critics who charge that *The Investigation* is impure with respect to genre: "What is involved is a
modern authorial strategy which some people may find intol-
erable, but which cannot be assailed with factual arguments,
since the demand for absolute purity of genrès is becoming
nowadays an anachronism in literature. The critics and readers
who hold Dick's 'impurity' with respect to genre against him
are fossilized traditionalists." Lem's mixture of genre may con-
found the "fossilized traditionalists" and it may cause the literary historian to pause as he attempts to categorize *The
Investigation* according to genre. But in symbolically demonstrating the conflict between two value systems, the maneuver
effectively presents Lem's recurrent theses about man in a
fresh, telling fashion.

4

Death with Full and Continuing Consciousness:

Return from the Stars

Although *Powrót z gwiazd* (*Return from the Stars;* 1961, 1980) is
one of Lem's earlier novels, it appeared only recently in the
United States. The plot in this book is one of Lem's least complex. Hal Bregg, an astronaut on the Prometheus Expedition to
the stars, has just returned to Earth, after 127 years in space,
yet he has aged only 10 biological years. The society to which
he returns has evolved markedly, so he must learn to cope
with significant changes. Instead of being an alien from outer
space or a human in outer space, Bregg is an alien in his original environment. In Lem's version of this twist in plot, he radically divests the astronaut of any familiar home base and
thoroughly destroys his frame of reference. In similar science-
fiction plots, the returning voyager is confused, but he usually
has some familiar custom, person, or setting to assist in the orientation process. Lem's plot is unusual because he provides
Bregg with virtually no people or devices by which to orient
himself until he has become reconciled to the necessity of trying to adjust to the new culture.

The story is narrated from Bregg's point of view. His values
reflect attitudes we associate with the twentieth century,
though the actual temporal setting is never specified. The
straightforward plot deals with Bregg's adjustment to this new

society as he passes through seven stages from confusion to a typically Lemian accommodation to change. Each of the first five stages is developed in a separate chapter.

In Chapter One, after leaving the safety of the carefully controlled reentry location (called "Adapt"), Bregg undergoes a confusing initiation on Earth. Changes in customs and technology leave poor Bregg almost helpless, as he is even unable to locate his contact person on Earth at the transportation station. Lem effectively draws the reader into Bregg's confusion by utilizing neologisms—primarily when the new humans give Bregg directions, talking to him about his "switch," the "polyduct," an "ulder," and the "rast" as means of transportation and referring to "Soamo," "Vuk," "real Ammo," "cosmolyte," "studios," and a form of cinematic art called a "real."

Hence, Bregg has difficulty in performing tasks as simple as moving from place to place. The first woman he encounters offers him "brit" and makes him feel like a very strange duck indeed. Since he hears someone refer to the twenty-seventh hour, he knows that this civilization tells time differently. Clothes are sprayed on and the currency system is entirely different. Technology has advanced to such a point that nearly anything a person wants is available. Lem reinforces the sense of confusion by offering absolutely no geographical orientation to Bregg's new environment, so the reader feels as dislocated as Bregg does.

Next Bregg learns about the technology, makes an initial adjustment to its wonders, and then seeks out tentative contact with a sympathetic new-style human—Aen Aenis. She is a star of the "real" who, unlike the other new-style humans, is unafraid of Bregg even though he has not been "civilized" by a process called betrization that renders the new-style human incapable of committing a violent act.

Bregg then concentrates on learning about the betrization process. He achieves a superficial understanding of it, but he is still drawn to violence that the future civilization no longer has the stomach to handle. Bregg subsequently has an affair with a new-style human—Eri Marger—who provides him with a full understanding of how thoroughly a betrizated human differs from Bregg. In a powerful recognition scene he realizes how crude and cruel yet vital the twentieth century is in comparison with Eri's refined, effete society.

Bregg also evaluates the advantages and disadvantages of the two societies, concerning himself mostly with what makes man human. Experiences with Eri and two surviving astronauts, Olaf and Thurber, lead Bregg to a provocative distillation of values from the old and the new societies. The experiences affect Bregg significantly, but as is characteristic of so many of his novels, Lem does not specify the precise nature of the protagonist's transformation and the ultimate consequences, so the reader is left to speculate on his own about man's future.

On one level the plot simply records Bregg's adjustment to this new society. On another level, though, the plot enriches the thematic issues concerning what it means to be human. Thus, the uncomplicated plot becomes essential to the embodiment of the themes in the novel. Seldom has Lem done a better job of enlivening his philosophical concerns through his plot.

The plot offers many technological advances in the opening two chapters and some space travel in the flashbacks, but the technology gives way to thematic issues, and the space travel never becomes anything more than a tool by means of which Lem is able to talk about where man is headed in the future. While the basic plot outline causes this novel to sound as though it were thoroughly steeped in science-fiction conventions, it has relatively little hardware.

Almost all of the thematic material about man's future focuses on the question of what it means to be human if man selects stability and the absence of fear as his highest priorities. Lem answers the question about man by describing Bregg and the new-style humans in a variety of situations that illuminate different aspects of the theme. The discussion of what it is to be human involves three segments: description of the old-style human (Hal Bregg), description of the new-style human (Aen and Eri, primarily) and evaluation of the advantages and disadvantags of each style.

As the story opens, the old-style human has become an alien on Earth who experiences profound isolation, but Lem implies that even when Hal left Earth for the lengthy expedition, he was already alienated. This profound sense of "otherness," then, is not peculiar to Hal's return from the stars (although the sensation intensifies at that moment). It is instead symbolic of the old-style human's individuality, a character trait that prompts him to seek new perspectives and solutions to puzzles long unsolved. The old-style human does not enjoy the problems connected with change, but he accepts change as a natural feature of life. Nor does he relish danger or risk, but he is able to cope with these experiences. He is capable of choice and senses that his freedom to choose is essential to his ability to explore for solutions. Much of the time he finds himself aware of a fundamental paradox—he is sick of risk, yet stability bores him so acutely as to evoke feelings of hatred. These traits culminate in a last attribute—Bregg is capable of the violence necessary for heroism.

The most salient element of the new society is the betrization process, which renders the whole community incapable of violence, including war and political strife. The dearth of violence eliminates fear and danger. When betrization is coupled with technological advances, virtually all instability and risk disappear. The new-style human lives in a harmonious, desire-free environment and experiences almost no change in his surroundings or life process. Thus, he is unaccustomed to adapting to new circumstances. Because anything he wants is provided, he becomes extremely passive, so even sex means little to the new-style human.

A corollary to the new-style human's passivity is his susceptibility to control by robots. Perhaps the most striking effect of betrization is the burgeoning sense of indifference and the waning concern for maintaining a sense of hope (hope seems irrelevant in a society that provides everything). The spirits of competition, and hence, heroism are being bred out of the race and with the disappearance of these attributes, this race is losing the curiosity necessary for exploration. These people have no sense of isolation or individuality and so perceive no reason to seek a better or different mode of existence. With the loss of all these features, Bregg fears, life will no longer retain the romance, adventure, and potential for change that provide him with his individual sense of meaning and his awareness of man's significance in the universe.

When Bregg evaluates the advantages and disadvantages of the two modes of existence, his preference for the old one is evident, but his open, friendly demeanor and his willingness to concede the positive aspects of the new culture provide an atmosphere conducive to an enlightening discussion of the issue. He notes, for example, that the rigorous screening process for choosing parents is eminently sensible because in twentieth-century culture we exercise more discretion before granting an individual permission to build a tree house than we do on his "right" to parent a child. Bregg is in complete accord as well with the drive to end war and international political conflict. Moreover, having lived for years with high levels of risk and insecurity, he finds the prospect of a stable, harmonious existence very appealing. Even if he is offended by the evaluation, he understands the new society's scathing rejection of the old-style culture, when it describes Bregg's world with terms such as "animality," "barbaric," "benightedness," and "cruelty." Additionally, he concedes that he can understand and handle the rationale for these changes when they are stated in general terms.

His problem with the new culture arises on two points. He has enormous difficulty when these principles affect him personally, and he is very uneasy when he realizes that the "immovable cornerstone of this world" is betrization. With the first, he lights on an unchangeable feature of human nature— self-interest. Many people are in favor of sweeping, significant social change so long as it does not touch them personally.

Were Bregg's reaction limited to provincial self-interest, his critics would perhaps be correct in their dismissal of him and his reaction to the new world. Bregg, however, is concerned with several larger philosophical issues: individual freedom, control, meaning, significance of the human species, and man's curiosity to explore his universe. In short, Bregg distinguishes between abstraction and particularity because in abstraction the generalizations fail to take into account the less obvious but nevertheless meaningful values involving the human soul, which he fears the new world has lost.

Betrization is a problem for Bregg because he perceives violence as an evil that regrettably accompanies the values he prizes dearly. But betrization, while eliminating that evil, simultaneously anesthetizes the soul. A complex chain of reactions may ensue. The demise of curiosity is accompanied by a loss of the heroic spirit through which an individual believes he is capable of new, courageous acts that lead to solutions. Loss of curiosity may also prompt loss of desire for change and loss of the flexibility necessary to anticipate and cope with unforeseen, uncontrolled new dangers in the environment. Control is essential to the freedom to choose; here, the rise of a powerful class of robots becomes an issue because it threatens man's freedom. Finally, in the existential framework, choice is critical if man is to maintain his sense of individual meaning and if he is to retain a sense of why the human species is unique.

This description of old-style and new-style men leads to a thorny problem for the reader: how to obtain an accurate sense of Lem's theme—about man—through his protagonist Hal Bregg. Reactions by reviewers George R.R. Martin and John Updike indicate how readers can be misled about the theme once they misunderstand Bregg's character and Lem's handling of generic traditions. Martin writes that Bregg is a "macho type who doesn't fit in a tranquil future. . . . That . . . is old, old, old." Martin then summarily dismisses Bregg, *Return from the Stars*, and Lem for having indulged in a cliché-ridden theme—the rejection of an effete futuristic culture. Likewise John Updike, ordinarily a perceptive reader of Lem's work, describes Bregg as a romantic lady-killer who makes Robert Mitchum and Richard Widmark "look courtly" and who "seems a bit brutal and thick even to us of the unbetrizated present." The mistake in these readings arises from the temptation to latch onto only one portion of Bregg's character, the narrator's perspective, and Lem's argument.

First, to an understanding of Bregg's character. While Bregg is romantic and finds he cannot forgo a measure of violence, he is also capable of sensitive, humane reactions that evoke reader empathy. For example, Bregg experiences touching bewilderment and helplessness not only in the face of new technology but also in the realm of love (with Eri). Moreover, when he discovers why Eri has decided to leave her husband and accompany him, Bregg reveals a genuine regret. " 'Eri,' I croaked, 'I . . . [Lem's ellipses] only now. I swear! Only now do I understand, only now, that you went with me because you were afraid.' "

The depth of Bregg's sorrow emerges when he attempts suicide in the aftermath of the disaster with Eri because of shame that he was not more perceptive about Eri's reason for leaving her husband, Seon. Bregg evaluates his own action very harshly:

> I had taken advantage of the situation so terribly and had forced her to go with me, and . . . everything had taken place on account of that—it was worse than anything I could have imagined, because it robbed me even of my memories, of that night [when Bregg and Eri made love], of everything. Alone, with my hands, I had destroyed all, through a boundless egoism, a lie that had not let me see what was at the very surface.

Bregg is also capable of renouncing his desire for Eri by leaving her behind and proceeding alone—a sacrifice for her that pains him enormously. Thus, Hal Bregg is a much more complex and vulnerable character than either Martin or Updike has indicated. No man capable of acknowledging his mistakes as Bregg does and of giving himself such a hard time should be dismissed as a mere macho type.

Lem's goal is, I believe, to point again and again to the paradox of man's plight. If he wishes to progress, he does so at great expense. Lem is not arguing that Bregg is unequivocally correct (narrative irony reinforces this point, as do the flaws in Bregg's character that make him anything but a hero); nor is Lem waiting anxiously for the advent of the betrization process. *Return from the Stars* is neither utopian nor dystopian literature. It is a sober examination of both sides of the issue.

Finally, misreadings arise because of Lem's manipulations of
utopian and dystopian forms. When generic distinctions were
more precise and authors observed them with some care, a
reader could assume that a readily discernible system of values
followed. Thus, in science fiction, a dystopian work could be
expected to reject a future world, and a utopian work would
embrace the values of the future culture. When Martin and
Updike hear Bregg acknowledging the inevitability of violence
in his life, perhaps they conclude that *Return* is a dystopian
novel. Unfortunately, this conclusion glosses over fine points in
Lem's presentation. Since he likes features of both worlds, he
refuses to compose a work that is clearly dystopian or utopian.
As with *The Investigation, Return from the Stars* defies classifi-
cation.

The significance of these misreadings for character and
genre emerges more sharply when we progress to Lem's conclusions about man's situation. Lem's position is embedded in
his depiction of Hal Bregg. As an astronaut, Bregg is subjected
to three psychological tests. "The Wringer" tests the candidate's capacity to withstand the physical stress of 400 g. "The
Ghost Palace" and "The Coronation" test the candidate's resources for dealing with emotional stress resulting from isolation in space and then indefinite waiting while being
suspended until rescue comes. "The Ghost Palace" indicates
that man is isolated but finds the reality of his isolation difficult
to accept. "The Coronation" alludes to the existential crisis
that arises when a person faces the nothingness of the universe. This latter test, Lem says, "went most against what lay
in a man—an utter annihilation, a doom, a death with full and
continuing consciousness." Most men subjected to "The Coronation" go insane, but Bregg survives it, indicating that he is
unusual. Lem imbues this test with significance that transcends the Prometheus Expedition, though. He links it to the
state of man in the new culture, where people lack desire, purpose, and meaning.

To remain fit for survival, twentieth-century man must be
alive emotionally. The new-world man as Lem describes him,
with his danger-free existence, becomes passive and indiffer-

ent to such a degree that he can be described as experiencing a "death with full and continuing consciousness." Thus, Bregg is that rare person who can act as a bridge between two cultures and who can begin to appreciate both. He is able to get along with the old-style pioneer astronauts, and he is able to love Eri. He can withstand the psychological stress of the three tests, but he can also achieve a beatific moment in which he and astronaut Tom Arder experience something he refers to as a "fusion of worlds."

He has no words with which to describe what happened to Arder and him, and when Eri asks what it was, he replies simply, "I don't know." He also indicates that the vision did not show up on their cameras, even though it was perfectly visible to them. Bregg is, in short, capable of a spiritual experience during which he realizes that there are places and events in the universe for which man has no explanation and which will, despite man's best efforts to understand them, remain unfathomable.

Indirectly, Lem has pointed Bregg toward a fundamental verity of psychology. The human psyche cannot distinguish between feelings of pain and feelings of pleasure, so if we suppress pain, we also cancel out the capacity for pleasure. Bregg can handle pain (the three tests) and so he is open to euphoria. The problem for the new-style man is that in eliminating pain, he has eliminated his capacity for pleasure and the sense of his soul. In the end, he has removed his source for meaning in life—hope that he can alter his feelings or state of being.

If Lem has depicted Bregg as a character who bridges both worlds—the old and the new—he has also brought us back to an essential paradox in man's plight: man yearns for a time when he will be free of danger, pain, and risk, but were he to achieve that state, his unhappiness would be so profound that he would repudiate this way of living. Lem highlights this paradox when he has Bregg quote Plato: "O wretched one—you will have what you wanted." Having created a character who bridges both worlds and a novel that contains both utopian and dystopian elements, Lem then refuses to indicate with any certainty where he thinks man is headed. In the moving conclusion to the novel, though, he shows Bregg discovering, amidst the change and the crumbling ruin of his world, an immutable place on Earth. The symbolic significance of this scene makes an obvious statement about the paradox in man's situation. To exclude either flux or immutability is to miss out on Lem's main point, for the essence of man lies in his planet's flux *and* in its immutability.

Since Lem utilizes Bregg's character as a means for launching much of his philosophical material, it is not surprising that Bregg's consciousness comes to dominate the first-person narrative. Lem develops Bregg fully as a conventional character and normal human being. The Lem trademark is already evident: one character's consciousness so dominates the story that the reader's impressions of other characters pale markedly. Even so, Eri and Tom Arder are fairly well-developed, major characters, whose positions on critical issues appear reasonable, even if different from Bregg's.

Lem's depiction of women is a potential sore spot, but the problem is not so serious as it initially appears to be. Bregg's rough treatment of Eri, the source of Updike's dismay, is certainly subject to charges of chauvinism, but it is important to note that the fear he induces in Eri is not limited to women characters. Bregg has the same effect on all of the new-style humans, because ordinarily in this world they need not deal with someone capable of violence (as Bregg is). Eri is, nevertheless, eventually shown to be an intelligent, sensitive person capable of feelings like those of an old-style human. Intellectually she is Bregg's equal (teaching him a great deal about the new style), and when Bregg finally transcends his need to control Eri, Lem depicts her as a coequal partner in a poignant love relationship. When Eri differs substantially from Bregg, it is not because she is a woman; the disparity results from her status as a new-style human.

The other two women in the story will present some problems for feminists, but once again, the issue is less serious than it first appears. Aenis comes off as a shallow, somewhat hardened woman, for whom a casual sexual encounter means little, an evaluation prompted by Bregg's dismay at her liberated attitude toward sex. Aen Aenis, a futuristic version of a Hollywood movie queen, is, in one sense, little more than a fulfillment of a male fantasy.

However, before condemning the characterization of Aen, we may find it useful to consider Lem's goal here. He utilizes character development symbolically to indicate Bregg's growth and adjustment to the new culture. The first people Bregg encounters barely register on his consciousness; they do not even have names. Then he meets Aenis, who impresses him at the moment because she is his first "guide" to the new world; she fades quickly, though, never to be mentioned again. Finally, with Eri, he develops a significant relationship and learns to adjust to life with an enormously different breed of humans. The progression in characterization from flat stereotype to fully developed individual reflects Bregg's evolving relationship with the new world.

Lem's characterization technique is not his only use of symbolism. In fact, *Return* is one of his richer novels in terms of symbol. Given his penchant for philosophy, the profusion of symbol is important. Writers interested in philosophical literature have always struggled with the problem of how to interweave the two disciplines, but for Lem the issue is particularly acute because he has, on occasion, justifiably been taken to task for allowing characters, especially Ijon Tichy, to slip off into philosophical jags that involve almost no literary elements such as human interaction. Often the science-fiction frame of a narrator's trip to another planet is the only literary device in a short story.

In *Return from the Stars*, Lem regularly creates visible, physical counterparts for the ideas he wishes to convey. For the betrization process, Lem has a drink, called "brit," to be administered to the "wild" individuals such as Bregg. The drinking of brit comes to be a focal point in Bregg's social encounters with new-style humans. The stars signify eternity, while the Prometheus expedition to the stars symbolizes old-style man's active spirit of curiosity and the desire for knowledge that prevails in the face of overwhelming odds. The new-style human's loss of interest in, and actual rejection of, the space program then becomes enormously revealing. Clavestra, a lotus-land Lem describes in terms not unlike those used by the Jamaican Tourism Bureau in ads in the *New Yorker* magazine, represents the lure of the new-style human existence.

Many of the symbols function as simple reflectors for abstract statements made elsewhere in the novel. Some of the symbols, however, provide a deeper function when they contribute to the development of an issue. One example involves a scar Bregg sustained from an accident during the trip to the stars. Eri notices it during a quiet, intimate moment and inquires about it. Initially Bregg is reticent, unwilling to discuss it, because as Eri perceptively observes, he is so acutely aware of their differences that he does not think she would understand what motivated him to get involved in the dangerous incident that caused the injury. Hence, the scar represents the violence and danger of the old-style life. It does more, though, than reflect Bregg's values. It also intensifies his sense of isolation.

Finally, Eri's persistence in asking about the scar prompts Bregg to open up to her about the adventure in space; this breakthrough contributes to the sense that Bregg and Eri can overcome their differences and develop an understanding of each other's values. In this respect, the scar functions as a catalytic symbol. The irony in philosophical terms is that the scar simultaneously highlights Bregg's isolation from, and his capacity for, intimacy with Eri, the representative new-style human. Symbolic technique of this sort abounds in *Return from the Stars*, so that on this point the novel is quite sophisticated.

Lem has indicated that he does not consider *Return* to be one of his better books. Although he has not been specific about what he considers weak, his subsequent movement away from conventional plotting and character development may be the key. *Return* does not pretend to be structurally inventive. There is ample reason, though, on another ground, for disagreement with Lem's assessment. As philosophical literature, *Return* is more effective than most attempts in the genre—including his own later works—because in *Return* he succeeds in using symbol to integrate idea and literature.

5

Belief in Cruel Miracles:

Solaris

So far, *Solaris* (1961, 1970), has been Lem's most popular novel. It has also received very positive critical response. Such a reaction is quite understandable, for in this book Lem retains the literary elements that attract a mainstream reading audience—strong plotting, tight narrative, traditional characterization, abundant symbolism, and love interest. Even though he turns to a new topic (man's reaction to an alien, incomprehensible force) and poses a long string of riddles for himself and the reader, the novel is warm and psychologically probing as only a few other Lem works are.

In this book a scientist named Kelvin joins an expedition to the planet Solaris. The planet has two suns and an unstable orbit that may be caused by a strange, highly-evolved, organic ocean that interacts with the human space travelers. The crew is comprised of four men, Kelvin, Snow, Sartorius, and Gibarian (who has committed suicide under suspicious circumstances before Kelvin arrives). Both Snow and Sartorius, laconic and secretive men, dissemble about the events that led to Gibarian's death. Gradually Kelvin learns about these events.

The ocean is capable of generating a physical "being" derived from each crew member's past. These "likenesses," referred to as "Phi-creatures," are biologically so similar to their human sources that Kelvin is able to prove the biological dissimilarity conclusively only when he performs a blood test under a microscope. The creatures also have two other interesting features: they appear capable of regeneration, and

49

they cannot tolerate being separated from their human sources. Kelvin's Phi-creature is Rheya, his wife, who committed suicide when he left her ten years earlier, a situation about which he feels very guilty.

The tale's three main plot lines develop from the mystery about Gibarian's suicide and the appearance of the Phi-creatures. The Kelvin/Rheya love story adheres closely to the tradition of the "realistic novel," despite the science-fiction trappings related to the reappearance of a dead person. Rheya's love for Kelvin and her agony about their potential separation (since she is not human) are immensely appealing, presenting as they do a male-female relationship missing from most of the other Lem books.

The second plot line concerns the ocean and its machinations in relation to man. The ocean is, it seems, alive and is involved in a never-ending process of transformation, "ontological autometamorphosis." No matter what experiments the scientists in Kelvin's crew attempt in order to understand the ocean or to outwit it, it outmaneuvers them. Moreover, the Phi-creatures appear to function as highly sophisticated spies, capable of knowing what their human counterparts are thinking.

The mystery lies in how the ocean works, because no apparatus for communication with the Phi-creature is visible. The Phi-creature's existence frightens and baffles the crew members, but the being itself is not the source of the anxiety because Rheya especially seems to be a victim who cannot control what happens to Kelvin and who seems as frightened and disconcerted as he is.

Terror for the human characters arises from the ocean's inability or unwillingness to communicate with man, so Kelvin, Snow, and Sartorius spend an inordinate amount of time trying to understand the ocean and its Phi-creatures, or, having failed to do this, attempting as Sartorius does to destroy that which strikes him as incomprehensible.

The third plot line consists mostly of Kelvin's reflections about puzzles related to the planet Solaris, such as what mimoids, symmetriads, and asymmetriads are and how the planet came to have two suns. A vast body of literature about Solaris has developed; Kelvin surveys the work by its most prominent thinkers. The third plot line is overshadowed in *Solaris* by the other two more traditional ones, but this predilection in the third plot line for expository experimentation and playing will eventually dominate Lem's work.

The narrative is tight and very engaging, even though the sorties into Solarian history appear to be digressions. It turns out that they are very important. Even the chapter titles indicate how traditional this novel is—"Arrival," "Solarists," "The Visitors," "Sartorius," "Rheya," "The Conference," etc. Almost all of the titles relate to an incident or a character. This taut, fast-paced plot is probably the key element in *Solaris*'s enormous appeal with the mass reading public because it presents a tragedy of well-intentioned people making mistakes and hurting one another. Mysteries and puzzles abound, but Lem solves enough of them to satisfy the average reader, even though a number of them remain to bedevil the most persistent lover of puzzles.

Lem uses a fair amount of scientific hardware, but he spends more time on imaginative creation of a hypothetical natural world—Solaris—and on beings that in traditional science fiction ought to be monsters. Instead, Lem transfigures them into philosophical problems. As will so often be the case, he is more concerned with theme, so that the hardware is the medium for the message rather than the message itself.

Thematically the book is rich and diverse. The dominant mood, though, derives from Lem's composition process. Although he often knew where he was headed as he wrote a novel, with *Solaris* he did not and so was writing spontaneously. More startling, however, is his statement almost twenty years after he wrote the book. Even then he was unable "to grasp just what it was I wanted to say in *Solaris.*" Later, in a 1979 interview, he specified his intention as one of epistemology: "This is a gnosseological drama whose focal point is the tragedy of man's imperfect machinery for gaining knowledge." Virtually all of the themes and variations in *Solaris* follow from this epistemological concern.

Lem's complex thematic statement develops as a response
to this question: How does man react if he is confronted with
an active, incomprehensible, uncommunicative, but benign
entity? Through the characters, Lem posits several reactions.
Gibarian commits suicide. Sartorius tries to destroy the alien
through "Operation Liberation"—like a Faust in reverse, says
Snow. Snow retreats into a schizoid shell, refusing to acknowledge the validity of his visitor and having decided to wait—es-
sentially unchanged—on Solaris for a possible solution to his
problems about the planet. He prefers this option to that of returning to Earth where he would be labeled insane for revealing what he knows.

These responses Lem clearly rejects in favor of Kelvin's, because each in its own way represents a capitulation or a refusal
to come to terms with the new world. Kelvin is transformed by
these events and (like Hal Bregg) experiences a spiritual, aesthetic vision at the novel's close. The major difference is that
Kelvin's apocalyptic vision includes an additional element—
love. Love, for Lem, provides tremendous creative power and
a source for admirable action by the main characters.

Kelvin passes through a number of trying experiences, including an encounter with a haunting woman, a confrontation
with a vast body of knowledge, a frightful bout over his sanity,
a horrifying yet wondrous dream, and a challenging exposure
to the natural world. Then, at the book's end, Lem relates the
Kelvin/Rheya love story to his main theme. He is not optimistic about love, observing: "The age-old faith of lovers and poets
in the power of love ... that *finis vitae sed non amoris* [the
end of life is not the end of love] is a lie, useless and not even
funny." However, despite this cynical statement, Kelvin returns to love as a source of hope, as he decides to stay on Solaris, with his memories of Rheya, in a balanced state that
involves hoping for nothing yet living in expectation, "in the
faith that the time of cruel miracles was not past." Lem depicts
dialectical tension, but he offers no indication that the positive
forces have even the slightest edge over the negative.

Darko Suvin, the editor of *Science-Fiction Studies*, adds a
useful insight concerning this dialectical balance. He suggests

that after acknowledging man's limitations, Lem also posits the necessity of trusting man because he will eventually accept his limitation and evolve toward a higher level of existence. Lem tantalizes the reader with hope, while still refusing to become either optimist or pessimist.

The key to man's confrontation with the alien force is his relation to the problem of knowledge. The huge body of obsessive Solarist literature develops because man has difficulty accepting a phenomenon that he cannot explain or understand. In other words, the existence of an inexplicable phenomenon is a visible, irritating reminder of the limits to man's knowledge.

The nonthreatening quality of the ocean contributes to the epistemological theme, because were the alien force an aggressive entity, this thematic concern would have to take a backseat to the adventure element of the plot. In *Solaris* the ocean does not present a clear danger, so Kelvin and other Solarist adventurers may approach it reflectively as a challenging object of study.

A significant corollary to a limitation in man's knowledge is a sense that man's anthropomorphism ought to be limited. Ironically and unfortunately, Lem finds, man still wishes to supersede his limitations and to believe that all the universe ought to be made "human." Lem seeks to indicate the folly of this perspective.

Another corollary develops from Lem's extension of the theme concerning the limits of man's knowledge. He argues that science is open-ended and history antieschatological. Man's limitations emerge in part because the sciences, Lem argues, are not absolute as some thinkers have argued, nor is history headed for a purposeful end, as Western thinkers so often contend. Lem reinforces these points in *Solaris* through his depiction of the field of Solaristics, which seems never to achieve a state of equilibrium. Here it becomes obvious that the material that appeared extraneous to the plot is in fact critical to Lem's thematic purpose. Lem reinforces the infinite nature of the universe—in literary terms—when he depicts the open-ended, dialectical balance at the novel's close.

Lem's assertions about science and history have implications
for theology as well. These become apparent in his discussion
of a god he describes as "imperfect." This god evolves, but he
"keeps increasing in power while remaining aware of his pow-
erlessness." Most importantly, though, this is a despairing god
who nevertheless persists, a god "who saves nothing, fulfills no
purpose—a god who simply is." This is the only kind of god
that an existential thinker could fathom. He exists without purpose.

This god offers an effective response to Sartre's dilemma
about explaining man's spirituality. Sartre denied the existence
of the traditional God. He argued that God has usually been
defined as the perfection of being toward which man strives.
Man, in turn, he says, has been defined by Western thinkers in
terms of his relation to this perfect God. Sartre sees man as an
imperfect being who must perpetually seek a goal that he cannot fulfill, from which he derives meaning. A being that
achieved a culmination of its purpose—that is, a state of perfection—would be a contradiction. Hence, Sartre argues, God
does not exist. Sartre is then faced with the problem of explaining man's spirituality and the persistence of the belief in the
existence of a god.

Lem offers an intriguing alternative when he describes the
imperfect god. This god, Lem contends, is not man, nor is it a
creation of man. The god develops and exists on its own terms,
independent of man. Lem links this god to the religious quality
of Solaristics as a field of study, arguing that modern man approaches the study of science and space as men formerly con-
templated the theological God—with a sense of mystery and
reverential awe.

The last major thematic concern is the psychology of man's
reaction to the alien force. Here the amorphous, experimental
quality of Lem's writing comes through. The emotional issues
surface primarily because of the nature of the Phi-creatures,
who develop from each man's subconscious desire and guilt.
Gibarian's creature is a giant Negress about which almost nothing is known, while Sartorius is perpetually badgered by some
scurrying critter, which he must repeatedly restrain to keep it

from escaping his chambers. Snow's "companion" is even more elusive, with little information available except that it exists and that it plagues him. The other space travelers' creatures are for the most part negative. Rheya, Kelvin's visitor, tortures him because he feels guilty about her suicide ten years earlier, but he also loves her deeply and has positive, even erotic feelings about her. In emotional terms, Kelvin's positive response to Rheya significantly overshadows the guilt complex.

The existence of these Phi-creatures leads Kelvin to question his own sanity, just as Earthlings in the past had questioned the sanity of a previous space traveler named Berton when he reported the existence of a giant child's face (his Phi-creature). Kelvin temporarily alleviates the concern about sanity when he performs independent experiments and discovers that the other crew members have similar experiences. Lem does little, though, to explain the presence of the Phi-creatures, the source of these beings in man's mind, or the madness that lurks in the shadow of this phenomenon.

A number of critics, most notably David Ketterer and Manfred Geier, have tried to explain the Phi-creature psychological puzzle. Geier developed an elaborate Freudian framework in order to argue that the phenomenon is a manifestation of Kelvin's schizophrenia. It is natural to seek an explanation for Lem's tantalizing puzzle, but Geier's interpretation raises as many serious problems as it solves. More critically, I would contend, it violates the spirit of Lem's intent in *Solaris*.

Geier's argument seems weak because Kelvin develops solid scientific proof for the existence of the Phi-creatures, other crew members corroborate his findings, and Berton wrote a chronicle in the past indicating a similar experience. Given these considerations, Geier can only support his thesis on schizophrenia by arguing that the whole narrative frame is a schizophrenic delusion of an unreliable, pathologically ill narrator. Too much internal evidence works to the contrary, indicating that in large measure Kelvin represents Lem's views.

Geier's approach prompts a faulty impression: that the problem is explicable in the terms of a logical social science such as psychology. Lem's stated goal (reiterated in several interviews) is to depict the limits of man's knowledge by offering an insoluble puzzle. How does the ocean develop Phi-creatures and what do they signify? In a sense, Geier attempts to explain what Lem sought to render inexplicable.

A final consideration with respect to Geier's position. If the reader concludes that Kelvin is mad, it becomes unduly easy to dismiss this character's confrontation with the limitation of man's knowledge. Only if the reader is convinced that Kelvin is sane will he participate fully in Kelvin's agonizing search for the meaning of the Phi-creatures.

If Geier's concern with pathology in *Solaris* has a legitimate application, it is with the epistemological theme. Commonly a person confronted with limitations experiences frustration, anxiety, anger, and fear. These emotions are manifested in all of the crew members to some degree, and in Gibarian and Sartorius the problem becomes acute. Kelvin, however, strikes me as eminently sane. His key problem is not self-perception, but how others perceive him. When man has been grappling with a problem he seems unable to resolve and one individual explores new frontiers in his quest for a solution, he often violates sacred beliefs and visions of the world. Berton is a fine example in *Solaris*. For his pain and courage he was rewarded with skepticism, ridicule, and accusations that he was insane.

Sanity, then, involves capitulation to accepted explanations of given phenomena, so that when an individual tests the limits of existing epistemological boundaries, questions inevitably arise about his sanity. Ultimately, with respect to the psychological realm in *Solaris*, Lem seems most interested in piquing the reader's curiosity while refusing to provide any answers.

Like the thematic development, symbolism in *Solaris* is rich and diverse. In fact, Lem probably renders symbol more central and compelling in this novel than in any other except for *His Master's Voice* or *Cyberiad*. The symbolism in *Return from the Stars* is integral and thorough with respect to the philosophical issues, but it is not nearly as engaging as that in *Solaris*. Some of the symbols are relatively clear and easily accessible in *Solaris*, such as the hindrances to communication-mirrors, glass, and doors. Most of the others, though, are provocative, implicit, and difficult to pin down. David Ketterer suggests that much of the symbolism relates to reproduction. For example, the spaceship is described in sexual, procreative terms; *Solaris* is a sun (pun on son), and the ocean, long a watery symbol of fertility, contains many references to female sexuality. Ketterer argues that this reproductive capacity is used in an illegitimate fashion by crew members and other humans in *Solaris* and that Lem is thereby emphasizing the fallacy in anthropomorphism.

Ketterer is correct to point out the negative aspect of this symbolism. However. he does not emphasize sufficiently its positive aspect. Lem is iust as intrigued by man's capacity for reproduction and creativity (referred to usually as invention, discovery, construction, or exploration) as he is repulsed by man's arrogance about his power. Hence, Ketterer's reading of individual symbols excludes a positive element that seems important to a balanced, complete understanding of Lem's purpose.

The Phi-creatures, another important symbol, do stand for man's erotic guilt as both Ketterer and Geier suggest. It is just as crucial, though, to note that Rheya is a "programmed mind," (Lem's phrase), who represents all machines. In *Mortal Engines* and *Cyberiad,* Lem devotes much more time to the relation between man and machine (cybernetics), but he offers a nascent presentation in his concern about Rheya's love for Kelvin. This is one of the few instances in which he considers heterosexual love in relation to cybernetics.

The two remaining significant symbols—the ocean and the planet Solaris—stand for the alien forces that indicate the limits of man's knowledge and the implacable silence of the universe. The ocean, in addition to its reproductive qualities, also evokes an aura of mystical spirituality. It reaches out and interacts with man, probing his mind via the Phi-creatures and wafting like a light breeze around the human subject it is investigating. Its mysteriousness ties it to the subconscious element of the human being. Finally, the ocean presents a challenge to man that frustrates while also elevating him so that he may pursue ever-higher goals.

On the other hand, the planet Solaris challenges and appeals

to the intellectual, scientific portion of man's being and to that
which is (despite being inexplicable) visible, physical, and susceptible to study by the Solarists in a way that the ocean is not.
Ultimately the Solarists represent the portion of man that becomes obsessed with knowing and with defying the limits of
knowledge. When these scientists exceed their boundaries unduly and lapse into anthropomorphism, Lem scorns them, but
at the same time, when their zeal feeds their desire to explore
space, Lem appears willing to acknowledge a measure of glory
in man's desire.

A final, relatively obscure symbol merits attention—the silence of the ocean and Solaris—because in later works it becomes one of Lem's most prominent symbols. On one level, the
silence alludes to nature's indifference about establishing contact with man, but on a deeper level, it stands for the radical,
fundamental nothingness of the universe. Lem's silence, in short,
signifies Camus's existential absurdity and Sartre's nothingness.

A thorough understanding of Lem's thematic intention also
requires an examination of his puzzles. He employs two
types—those related to plot and those related to philosophical
issues. Usually he poses a problem, such as who the Phi-creatures are—and then he allows the reader to experience vicari-
ously the protagonist's struggle with the dilemma. Even the
veteran Lem reader cannot be certain which puzzles will be
solved and which left hanging as a reminder of man's limitation and fallibility. In *Solaris*, the one important unresolved
concern is what becomes of Rheya after Snow "handles the
problem."

With philosophical puzzles the situation is somewhat different. In many instances involving the plot puzzles, Lem offers a
solution. With philosophical puzzles the reader is ordinarily
able to make sense of at least a portion of the conundrum. For
example, some cognitive sense about the ocean and the planet
Solaris is available. However, in a significant number of instances Lem offers tantalizing leads but no hard evidence or
scientific explanation. Kelvin knows that at times the ocean is
aware of his presence and that at other times it is not, but he

does not know why or how, whether it is lack of interest or lack of awareness.

Ultimately Kelvin learns, as critic David Lavery remarks, that the "planet-ocean remains an unfathomable mystery." Kelvin will come to understand this natural force only when he yields to "its sway." The key to this philosophical puzzle is that man must eventually learn in certain situations to forgo control, give in to the subconscious aspects of his personality and world. Here the unique feature of Kelvin's reaction at the end emerges—he is willing as no other crew member is to go with the mystery and the chaos of the ocean/planet and, in the process of yielding "control" over his destiny, to renounce his anthropomorphic vision of the universe. The possibility, of course, is that Kelvin will learn of an entirely new mode of being, which the other control-obsessed crew members (i.e., typical human beings) could never entertain. Despite his willingness to yield control, he remains on Solaris, a point that will become important in a comparison with *The Invincible*.

Lem also poses numerous insoluble puzzles about physical features of Solaris, such as the meaning of mimoids, asymmetriads, symetriads, the agilus, fungoids, and extensors, phenomenon for which there is no earthly counterpart. Mimoids, it seems, are "wave formations of thousands of tons of water . . . in which objects external to the ocean are imitated within its textures." The "visions" within the mimoid are fluid—visible, available for examination—yet transient and inscrutable. Lem offers a wealth of additional physical detail about the mimoid and the other phenomenon but little else about their meaning, function, or etiology. Once again, Lem provides puzzles to tease and provoke, not to solve.

With respect to the* puzzle of the Phi-creatures, Kelvin learns several things about them. They are capable of human emotions and experience a painful panic if their source leaves them. Their blood is not identical with human blood, they regenerate injured body parts (therefore, are not mortal in the usual sense), and their skin is soft, like that of a newborn child. Lem leaves a host of unexplained issues, though: how are these

beings created, how can they get inside a man's mind, and why
are they so painfully dependent? The Phi-creatures function as
some of the more interesting aliens in science-fiction literature
precisely because they are so human without being humans.
For this very reason, however, they are all the more disturbing
when Lem explores questions about what it means to be a man.

The last important puzzle concerns the dreams that Kelvin
experiences. He is convinced that the ocean is visiting him to
prompt the nocturnal visions. Lem offers no explanation for the
origin or purpose of the dreams. However, Kelvin changes because of them. He experiences horror about the potential violence and evil in the universe, a horror much like what
Nietzsche describes in *The Birth of Tragedy* as the Dionysian
force. Kelvin's experience involves a grotesque dream vision
that recurs several nights in a row. His insight is visual, but later
it becomes nonvisual. Then he feels himself "being invaded
through and through, I crumbled, disintegrated, and only emp-
tiness remained. Total annihilation was succeeded by such terror that its memory alone makes my heart beat faster today." At
this point, the sequence of dream experiences has made possible
a thorough restructuring of the protagonist's being.

Kelvin then enters a second phase of transformation, wherein he has a waking vision of magnificent birds. The second portion of this revelation comes not as a vision but as an
experience when he leaves the spaceship at the novel's end to
explore Solaris for himself—alone. This segment of the process
takes place after some interval, but Kelvin emerges from the
dreams to have a spiritual experience while challenging a natural phenomenon on his own terms. Kelvin's solitary experience echoes those of Hans Castorp in Mann's *Magic Mountain*
and Zarathustra in Nietzsche's *Thus Spoke Zarathustra.*

With this comparison to Mann and Nietzsche, the significance of Kelvin's insistence on going out alone emerges. Kelvin had to leave behind the limited human beings such as
Snow in order to confront himself and to take on the existential challenge of being open to change (i.e., choice), just like
Castorp and Zarathustra on their mountains. In Kelvin's case,
the change is to accept a new posture and a new world in

which man is not supreme and must instead wait expectantly while believing in "cruel miracles." The dream, by whatever inexplicable means, has prompted an actual existential reshaping of the novel's hero, not to render him glorious, but to render him capable of surviving life in the new world.

It may be obvious by now that Lem follows his usual characterization strategy in *Solaris*—an intense narrative consciousness dominates, while most other characters fade sharply. Kris Kelvin is that imposing consciousness who passes through a tragic rite of initiation, but two figures emerge from shadowdom to develop into particularized characters—Snow and Rheya. Lem is sketchy on Snow's background, but the character's emotions and his views develop fairly well, especially concerning the wisdom he has gained through his earlier experience with Phi-creature visitors.

Rheya is an interesting character because her realness fluctuates. At times she is extremely vivid and convincing, particularly when she expresss her love for Kelvin and her agony over their differences. At other times she seems flat and stereotypical (that is, not human). Of course, since she is not human, Lem may have intentionally depicted her in this manner. She may also have fluctuated in her humanness and depth as a character because Lem was trying to portray her as a reflection of Kelvin's consciousness, since his narrative vision was the medium for all other detail in the story. That is, when Kelvin is interested in her, she is live and real (after all, she is a creature of his making), and when he is preoccupied with other issues such as Sartorius's attack on the ocean, she fades. Anomalies in the depiction of Rheya aside, several characters other than Kelvin emerge as unusually warm, significant individuals.

The depiction of Rheya may pose some difficulties for feminists—similar to those with Eri and the other women in *Return from the Stars*—for occasionally Rheya seems to be little more than an embodiment of an erotic male pipedream. Lem redeems her, however, in the depth and the poignancy of his portrait. Rheya's emotional pain over her circumstance and physical condition is so alive and plausible that she emerges eventually as a significant foil for Kelvin.

Reservations about characterization aside, *Solaris* is nevertheless an admirable novel. The plot is innovative. Lem discusses themes that show up elsewhere in his canon, such as communication with aliens, anthropomorphism, epistemology, and sanity. He devises several challenging, enigmatic symbols, including the ocean and the Phi-creatures. The ever-present puzzles are intriguing. The characterization is solid. No one element is vastly different from or remarkably superior to its counterpart in the other novels, yet *Solaris* stands as one of Lem's best works. Why? In part, this is because he executes a large number of elements more effectively here than in other books. More importantly, though, the novel has a genuine human warmth and a spontaneity in plotting that some of Lem's other novels augur but do not deliver quite so sensitively. *Solaris* has the human touch that involves not only the mind but the heart.

6

My Case:

Memoirs Found in a Bathtub

Pamiętnik znaleziony w wannie (*Memoirs Found in a Bathtub;* 1961, 1973) uses a futuristic narrative frame and a smattering of scientific technology, but it is primarily a satiric/grotesque depiction of a bureaucracy gone wildly awry. Lem opens the novel with a narrative frame presented by an unspecified individual from an advanced civilization. This person reports the discovery of an ancient relic, a common science-fiction device, called "Notes from the Neogene," dating from the "very close of the Prechaotic, that period of decline which directly preceded the Great Collapse." The Collapse occurred because a country called "Ammer-ka," noted for its "fanatic devotion to the deity Kap-Eh-Taahl," experienced "papyralysis," a crisis that led to "historioparalysis."

The combination of the futuristic setting and the humorous spelling of key words creates a sense of "safe" distance from twentieth-century culture. This allows Lem, the Polish East Bloc writer, to skewer with exquisite precision not just the American social structure (actually a secondary concern for him), but more importantly the ideological clash between East and West and the problems caused when the bureaucracy becomes a pervasive social phenomenon in any technologically advanced culture.

The most notable archaelogical discovery by this advanced culture—in the year 3146—is the Third and Last Pentagon (the setting for the "Notes from the Neogene"), a structure that had been written off by residents of this futuristic society as a figurative concoction by the last faithful survivors of the capitalistic era. This Pentagon structure, which housed a community of "Priests and warriors of Kap-Eh-Taahl," existed in "absolutely hermetic isolation" and was referred to as "the Building." The absolute isolation of the Last Pentagon becomes a crucial detail in the story.

The plot within the frame (that is, the "Notes," which are referred to informally as the "Memoirs Found in a Bathtub") offers one nameless individual's chronicle of his grotesque experience with the Building after he has been told that he has a "Special Mission" to perform. During the course of the attempt to discover and carry out his mission, the narrator encounters nearly every bureaucratic obstacle created—deliberately or inadvertently—by man. The material within the narrative frame draws substantially on two Kafka stories, *The Castle* (primary source) and *The Trial* (secondary), as Lem's narrator concerns himself with "his case," and as he wanders down seemingly endless corridors, discovering that no one knows what his mission is or how to solve his case. But while the tone in Kafka's stories is dominantly nightmarish (with a humorous touch), Lem's story creates a far more balanced blend of humor, satire, and nightmare.

Lem employs a flashback from the futuristic frame to a contemporary setting, but otherwise he develops the story in a simple, chronological fashion, using an episodic structure that resembles an interior picaresque. The narrator wanders through the landscape within the Building instead of across the countryside, indicating the limited scope of his hermetic world and the pervasive control the bureaucracy exercises over the individual.

The thematic issues in this novel range widely: existential concerns, sanity, conformity, the nature of truth, and the struggle between warring ideologies. Lem's foremost concern in *Memoirs*—the individual's response to a monolithic, insular bureaucracy—raises two thorny related questions. Is this novel existential? How is the reader to interpret the Building/Antibuilding antithesis?

Memoirs contains all of the elements that we associate with existential literature. The narrator, ordered in a written notice to assume a Special Mission (the "Project" in Sartre's existential frame), initiates his undertaking confident that he has a mission and that he will be able to fulfill it. Immediately, though, he encounters snafus in determining what that assignment involves. General Kashenblade assures him that he has a mission, but, when pressed about detail, notes that words fail him and adds only that the mission is "extremely hazardous." Lt. Blanderdash, the next bureaucratic obstacle, asked about specific instructions on the mission, offers the following "illuminating" tidbit: "It's difficult, complicated . . . [Lem's ellipses] unusual too—I'm sorry, your name?"

Next, Major Erms offers a hint that the narrator's instructions may be in code. By now the narrator is shaken and comments: *"I was beginning to doubt the very existence of the instructions themselves."* This snafu subsequently leads the narrator through the usual elements of existential angst. He loses the sense that his actions are consequential, fears the void or the nothingness of an absurd world, develops traits of paranoia, and asserts that there are no answers to life's difficult questions. He even attempts to flee his problem and begins to believe that nothing is expected of him and that action has no place in this world. Worse yet, he develops an intense awareness of chaos in the universe, senses isolation, and, finally, as he withdraws from involvement in this hermetic society, develops a self-centered obsession with his own case.

That existential elements are present in *Memoirs* is obvious. Not so obvious is how Lem wishes the reader to respond to them. It is tempting when concentrating on one aspect of the book—the parallels between *Memoirs* and Kafka and Sartre—to assume that *Memoirs* is an existential novel. However, a broader reading of the text reveals that Lem makes extensive use of parody and satire on other topics, so it seems likely that he intends to include existentialism in his satiric net.

A partial list of topics for satire indicates just how pervasive Lem's barbed wit becomes. He pokes at capitalism, socialism, bureaucratic rules on paperwork, fear of others and of life, division of labor, government secrecy and coding systems, the

military bureaucracy, the bureaucracts who administer the
military bureaucracy, and the secretaries who serve the bureaucrats. The irony implicit in the satire also points to the irony in the title of the novel. It is difficult to remain completely
serious when the reader recalls where the record of this ostensibly "heroic" existential quest is located—in a bathtub.

A passage from the text, describing an encounter between
the narrator and a secretary, is typical of the tongue-in-cheek
atmosphere that Lem fosters throughout the story:

> "But you have no appointment," she repeated over and over
> again. I demanded an appointment. But that was out of the
> question, she said; I would have to submit my petition in tripli-
> cate through the proper channels, then get the necessary signa-
> tures. But my Mission was Special, Top Secret. I tried to explain
> without raising my voice; it could only be discussed in absolute
> privacy. But she was busy with the phones—answering with a
> word or two here, pressing a button or two there . . . and hardly
> seemed aware of my existence.
>
> After an hour of this I swallowed my pride and began to
> plead with her. But pleading didn't have the least effect, so I
> showed her the contents of my folder. . . . I might have been
> showing her old newspapers for all the response this produced.
> She was the perfect secretary: nothing existed beyond the nar-
> row limits of her routine. Driven to desperate measures, I let
> out a stream of terrible confessions . . . about how I had unwit-
> tingly caused the suicide of the little old man . . . I began to in-
> vent things. . . . I demanded the worst—arrest, dishonor—I
> screamed in her ear. But she waved me away as if I were a fly,
> and continued to answer the phone with complete indifference.

If existentialism is to be taken as an alternative to these zany
snafus with the bureaucracy, rather than as one more subject
for Lem's satire, this philsophical option must come across in a
serious manner. It simply does not. The narrator's pursuit of
his mission and his concern with his case, while depressing at
times, becomes ludicrous and grotesque. His existential crisis
takes place in the bathroom, where the memoirs are later
found. Moreover, four pages before the novel's end, in the

midst of the narrator's frenzied queries about whether he is insane, Lem notes that the Building smiled at the narrator. In this light, it is necessary to conclude that *Memoirs* works as a subtle spoof on existentialism.

That Lem's satire is all-inclusive, as he takes a poke at socialist bureaucracies as well as at capitalism and existential thought, leads into an explanation of the otherwise troublesome Building/Antibuilding antithesis. Initially, the Building appears to stand for the bureaucracy and nothing else. Lem describes its physical structure and its traits like those of a living being, while depicting a particular bureaucracy. When Lem later posits the presence of an Antibuilding, it seems likely that he is creating a force opposed to the establishment and to bureaucracy. But then he indicates that the Antibuilding is just as mired in bureaucracy as the Building is. Moreover, he deliberately obscures the precise nature and function of the Building and the Antibuilding, noting only that each "shifts" in response to movement by the other. The key to interpreting the meaning of these two forces emerges from a little ditty:

> Hey, the Building, hey!
> What makes the Building stay?
> The Antibuilding makes it stay!
> Hey!

In specific terms, the antithesis represents the antagonism between the East and the West, between Communism and Capitalism, but on a universal level the antithesis suggests the see-saw dialectic between any set of competing ideologies. Lem seems uninterested in taking sides with either ideology, appearing far more concerned with the negative effects of the Cold War tension on all persons involved in it. He damns bureaucracies in both the East and the West. They foster facelessness, frustration, confusion, codes that lead to undue secrecy, inaction, rigidity, and loyalty oaths. Moreover, no one possesses an essential overview on how the system works, so everyone must cope with obstacles, isolation, humorlessness among the bureaucrats, and assumptions of infallibility.

Lem makes extensive, relatively obvious use of symbols, the notable exception being the Building/Antibuilding antithesis. "My case" stands for an individual's existential situation in the world and the hermetic isolation of the Last Pentagon for the insularity of the bureaucracy. A razor suggests the narrator's flirtation with suicide, tests and codes refer to the secrecy and paranoia that the bureaucracy engenders, and endless corridors point out to the labyrinthine nature of bureaucratic structure.

Lem's characterization technique is interesting because he utilizes it to symbolize man's limited perspective on events taking place around him. With the exception of the narrator, Lem renders all of the characters as caricatures. When a character is fleshed out to any extent, the individualistic trait is provided only as a means of presenting that person as a grotesque. This happens in the case of an old man whose only distinguishable feature is a little finger that will not stay in place, a symbol of ostentation, haunting the poor fellow even after his death when, in the casket, the pesky finger on the corpse perks up just enough for the narrator to notice it.

The narrator, unlike these grotesques, is depicted in a traditional manner, from a limited, first-person perspective. The only realistic, plausible human reactions in the novel come from him. Lem thereby points to the fact that every person perceives the world in a radically egocentric manner. All that can be conveyed fully, Lem seems to suggest, in any single character's perspective is his own understanding of the event. Any other perspective is rendered one-dimensional by the single character's inclination to interpret signs, actions, and words in a fashion that will advance his own purposes.

Since the other figures in *Memoirs* are caricatures, the narrator provides the only character development. The change actually involves deterioration, as the narrator loses his initial zeal and slips into an increasingly depressed state of mind, made virtually inevitable because of the hermetic isolation of the Pentagon. It is important to note, though, that the narrator is only the implied author and that his perspective does not represent Lem's. Lem's perspective lies mostly in the material from the narrative frame. While he utilizes black humor to depict the Cold War era, his satiric inversion, his humor, and the narrative frame from the year 3146 create sufficient distance from the narrator's hapless plight and doleful perspective that the reader may emerge from the world of the hermetically sealed Pentagon with a sense of measured optimism—somehow, Lem implies, mankind will survive.

Lem's main point in *Memoirs* is not to raise stock science-fiction issues. He utilizes the science-fiction narrative frame primarily as a means of instilling hope and as a rationale for launching an amusing, provocative, satiric, occasionally depressing tour de force on Cold War ideologies, bureaucracy in the 1950s, and existentialism.

7

The Realm of Perfected Death:

The Invincible

With *Niezwyciężony i inne opowiadania* (*The Invincible;* 1964, 1973), Lem produces yet another variation on his recurrent concern for man's situation in the universe. As in *Solaris,* he generates a plot about how man reacts in the presence of an alien force. He also indulges in his passion for puzzles, prompting Ursula Le Guin to describe it as a mystery novel. At the same time, *The Invincible* represents a significant variation in Lem's art, in both literary technique and theme. *Invincible* is redolent with science fiction hardware and is given over to plot—instead of philosophical analysis—as few other Lem novels are. The difference is most apparent when one character interrupts a prolonged discussion of a mystery by stating: "Whether the cloud's behavior is triggered by conscious mental activity or not is completely immaterial at this point. . . . Our present task is not to find a single hypothesis that will answer all our problems, but rather one that will guarantee us maximum possible security in the course of our stay on this planet."

The puzzles in *The Invincible* are also handled much differently from the way they are in *Solaris.* Here Lem solves most of the puzzles, and he chooses those that involve active agents rather than existing passive phenomena. He even depicts a significantly different type of alien force.

The development of the theme in *Solaris* and *The Invinci-*

ble runs along different lines as well. *Solaris* combines philosophical exposition with action, while *The Invincible* begins with an overlapping thematic concern—reaction to an alien force—but *The Invincible* also includes a fairly well-developed presentation on a topic that is inchoate in *Solaris*—evolution of machines (one aspect of cybernetics).

In this novel a space navigator named Rohan is on a mission with the *Invincible* spaceship to Regis III in search of the *Condor*, a missing ship which left no evidence of its demise save a garbled radio message. When the *Invincible* finally locates the *Condor*, its scientists are baffled initially by the condition of the remains. The ship has, it turns out, been attacked by a Black Rain variously referred to as "The Cloud," "metallic particles," and "flies." Once the *Invincible* crew discovers the power invested in the Black Rain, it begins to understand the significance of a "city of ruins" Rohan locates. (It turns out to be an impenetrable growth of discarded machinery that the rain has somehow rendered nonfunctional.) The balance of the plot is devoted to adventures with the metallic rain.

The rain has a number of intriguing properties. The diamond-hard, metallic, Y-shaped particles are capable of flight. They lack rationality and the ability to seek out new intelligence, but they have a memory-storage facility that allows them to learn from previous situations and upon which they can call in times of danger. Approached individually, they are innocuous. However, once they join as a unit, they are capable of elaborate self-protection movements; their swarming capacity renders them superbly mobile and adaptable in defensive maneuvers. And they can also attack. Through evolution they have learned that the most efficient means of handling enemy forces is not to kill but to render them amnesiac and helpless in a state of virtual infancy. They are extremely sensitive to movement of forces within their field of range, but if an alien remains perfectly still, he can exist unmolested in their midst.

The Black Rain differs from *Solaris*'s alien ocean in several important ways. It is most noticeably an active agent capable of, and at times intent upon, conquering aliens. Hence, it poses a visible threat that the ocean and the planet Solaris did not. Without the threat of bodily harm on Solaris, Kelvin was able to study and even become involved with the silent alien and to feel sympathy for it. Such is not the case in *The Invincible,* where Rohan must either devise a means to conquer the Black Cloud or retreat before it. Peaceful coexistence is not an option. Thus, adventure dominates *The Invincible* because the alien is so different from man.

The plot passes through four distinctive stages that dovetail nicely with Lem's thematic concerns about man's relation to machines. Initially, the element of the unknown prompts fear and expectancy, as the crew of the *Invincible* investigates nearly a dozen mysteries—for example, where is the lost *Condor,* what happened to it, how does the metallic rain work, how does it render men amnesiac, and what is the city of ruins? As Lem's characters solve this series of mysteries, they relax enough to be able to hypothesize about the rain. Thus far, Lem is following a pattern he has often used in the past.

Next, though, he has the crew launch a foolhardy attempt at conquest that precipitates a futile, devastating conflagration between the human warriors (and their technology) and the Cloud. When it becomes apparent that the crew members and their normal weapons cannot prevail, the ship's captain, Horpach, orders an attack by their huge and purportedly invincible tank, called the Cyclops. The ensuing battle between the Cyclops and the Cloud develops into an extraordinary spectacle that teaches Rohan and the *Invincible* crew a painful, humiliating lesson.

Finally, Rohan goes back into the battle carnage for a last-ditch effort to rescue "misplaced" crew members. During the lonely mission, Rohan comes to terms with man's limitations, as have Bregg, Tichy, and Kelvin before him. This time, however, he does not attempt cohabitation. He not only preaches retreat but also advises that man should leave the planet, never to intrude again—not just because it presently appears to be an insuperable force but because Rohan has come to respect its integrity. He has decided that there are places man does not belong. Rohan's venture away from the ship, like Kelvin's in

Solaris, develops into an existential struggle—on a physical and emotional level—through which man's capacity is vigorously tested.

The tight plot in *The Invincible* contains very few digressions or secondary thematic concerns. Plot is the dominant element of this novel, but for some reason, difficult to explain, it is not as captivating as the plot in *Solaris* or in other Lem works. Perhaps the simplicity and the straightforward character of the Cloud's attack is less provocative than the psychological probing by the Phi-creatures capable of eliciting love, guilt, and erotic sexual reactions. On the other hand, the abundant hardware is well-integrated and, according to Ursula Le Guin, "elaborate and impeccable," while the science is "solid and central."

The thematic scope of *The Invincible* is more narrowly focused than it is in *Solaris.* Here Lem explores two interrelated issues: man's invincibility and capacity for heroism; and man's relation to an evolving artificial intelligence. The question of man's invincibility is closely related to the issue of the limitations of his knowledge. This time, though, Lem concentrates on man's potential in an adventurous contest with a tangible, attacking foe.

A cybernetic theme introduces a new feature into an old topic—that is, man's relation to the universe—but most striking in *The Invincible* is the presentational mode for the theme of man's invincibility. Lem confronts his protagonist with an old-fashioned, threatening foe, which engages him in a battle scene of Homeric proportions. The question now shifts from whether man will prevail (anthropomorphism) to whether man will survive attack by a hostile force. Somewhat unusually for Lem, this shift aligns *The Invincible* with traditional science fiction.

Lem approaches the subject of man's invincibility or dominance in the universe by calling attention first to human technological advances in the opening "Black Rain" chapter. He then depicts a crew confident of its capacity to handle whatever difficlties it may encounter.

In the ensuing incidents, Lem develops a two-part approach

to the question of man's invincibility. Much to the crew's astonishment, the Cyclops, representative of the apex of man's technological advancement, meets its match in the Black Rain. For the first time Lem goes beyond mocking man's pretensions about dominating the universe and depicts the defeat of his hardware. Put another way, he cuts man down to size more ruthlessly than usual. The battle scene between the Cyclops and the Cloud receives extraordinarily thorough treatment, a full chapter of 20 pages in a novel that runs only 183 pages. The crew watches from the distance as the supposedly invincible Cyclops lumbers into battle, reminiscent of the fight scenes in *The Iliad* where observers report on the magnificent deeds of heroic warriors. The crew's dismay as the Cyclops meets its match shifts from horror to fear when the Rain manages to convert the Cyclops completely and turns it against its constructors so that the crew is forced to protect itself from the Rain *and* its own technology.

Having posited the fallibility of man's technology, Lem turns to the more basic issue, the survival of the physical man. Here he reverts to his standard view. Man is tenuously balanced between foolish pride and moments of genuine glory. This portion of Lem's theme arises in the depiction of the protagonist Rohan, who disparages the attitudes of his fellow crew members:

> How foolhardy, how ludicrous this "victory at any price," this "heroic persistence of man," this obsession with retaliation for the death of their companions, who had perished only because they themselves had sent them to their deaths . . . [Lem's ellipses] We were simply not cautious enough, we relied too much on our powerful weapons. We made mistakes, and now we must take the consequences. We and no one else are responsible.

Having used Rohan to criticize man's folly, Lem then casts him as the test material on the question of man's capacity for survival. Ironically, the character most skeptical about man's capacity for heroism is the only individual who accomplishes a singular, heroic action.

Lem refines his thematic statement on man primarily through the struggle Rohan experiences at the end of the book. The captain, Horpach, manipulates the situation so that Rohan feels responsible for seeing what he can do to rescue four men who might have survived the catastrophe. Rohan's encounter with the carnage and his struggle against the natural elements prompt an existential crisis. Rohan has confirmed that three of the four men are dead. If he is to confirm the fate of the fourth man, he will seriously deplete his oxygen supply and thereby take a potentially fatal risk merely to fulfill his duty and to soothe his conscience. Or he could return safely to the ship. Lem does not indicate whether Rohan finds the fourth man, but he follows this moment with a detailed account of a painful trek back to the ship, during which Rohan is in mortal danger.

Nearly exhausted, Rohan has one of the by now stock aesthetic experiences for Lem's protagonists: he sees "a mirror image of the bottom of the valley" in a mountain range, from which emerges a "gigantic human figure whose head projected into the darkness." Lem has a simple explanation for this seemingly supernatural event. It happens because of certain light conditions in the Alps which prompt a reflection of a person standing there—a "colossal shadow in the clouds." He argues that the incident has no symbolic meaning. Its placement, however, makes it difficult to dismiss the incident. Rohan has been through a harrowing, precarious trial and has achieved his aesthetic vision. Surely, Lem's denial notwithstanding, the colossal shadow may be read as an allusion to man's potential, particularly because it is placed at a critical juncture—five pages from the novel's end.

Given the Cyclops's (and thereby the crew's) humiliating defeat and Rohan's skepticism about man's capacity for heroism, his fate offers an interesting reconstruction of Lem's statements (through Rohan) earlier in the novel on the subject of heroism. During his "rise" here at the novel's end, Rohan's fear of the Cloud dissipates and he even manages to outwit it by remaining still. Thus, by the novel's conclusion, Rohan has become a figure of heroic proportions, even if his accomplishment is not heroic by traditional standards. One of Lem's comments in *Mortal Engines* is useful here. He says that "science explains the world, but only Art can reconcile us to it." Rohan's experience in the mountains of Regis III reconciles him to man's limitations.

The final significant aspect of Rohan's trek is his symbolic return to the ship, where Lem reasserts the tenuousness of man's survival and his potential for glory. At this point the description of the *Invincible* spaceship represents Lem's sentiments about man. He describes Rohan's approach:

> With unsteady, exaggerated strides, stiffly drawn up to his full height, his fists clenched in order to suppress the unbearable trembling of his fingers [caused by physical exhaustion], he strode straight towards the twenty-storey-high [sic] spaceship that, bathed in a blaze of light, stood outlined before the paling sky. There it towered, majestic as ever in its motionless grandeur—as if it were indeed invincible.

Lem juxtaposes tenuousness with simple grandeur. His subjunctive formulation perfectly crystallizes his thematic point— as if it were indeed invincible. Man is not invincible, but he is worthy of respect.

Lem's second, related thematic topic is cybernetics. Within that field he takes up man's relation to artificial intelligence and its evolution. In keeping with the thematic technique in the rest of the novel, Lem does not include much analysis of the two subdivisions of cybernetics. For the most part, he simply derives a plot that involves cybernetic issues. In the next two books, *Mortal Engines* and *Cyberiad,* he will work out the ramifications of cybernetics in some detail.

In *The Invincible,* the material on the evolution of artificial intelligence is concentrated in chapters entitled "In the Ruins" and "Lauda's Hypothesis." The former chapter describes a city of "undefinable formations" several stories high. When the buildings were destroyed they formed webs of matter that eventually created an overgrowth much like that in a jungle. The city is dead and apparently useless. In this expository chapter, Lem offers no answers to questions about the city's origin or demise. Clearly, though, the location was not occupied by humans.

In "Lauda's Hypothesis," an older biologist among the crew, named Lauda, advances a theory about the city of ruins that lays out the basic cybernetic issues. He suggests that inhabitants from a Lyre constellation spaceship may have crashed on Regis III. The only survivors were robots that somehow managed to reproduce themselves and engage in an evolutionary battle against living things and other forms of artificial intelligence. The robots conquered living forces, while the evolutionary struggle of the artificial intelligences was between those with the ability to miniaturize and those that settled into one place. The miniaturization trait defeated the stationary; thus, the mobile, tiny rain pellets are still active, while the stationary mechanisms are the metallic forest in the city of ruins.

The Rain has no rational capacity; it does have a superb memory bank. Lauda surmises that the Rain, then, can adapt but not think. He sees no prospect for man to defeat the Black Cloud and insists that the best course for the crew is to retreat from Regis III. If Lauda's hypothesis is correct, the future for man is, he concedes, very bleak indeed. His theory addresses a number of critical issues. He says that the simpler rather than the more complex mechanism won out because it did not need its creator the way the complex mechanism did. Lauda also points to the virtual indestructibility of this system. The other scientists raise additional provocative questions about how the Cloud learns, how it adapts to forces it has not previously encountered, whether it is conscious, and how it communicates between units.

Lem's presentation on cybernetics has advanced since *Solaris*, when he simply mentions the issue. In *The Invincible* he offers a full chapter of description and a full chapter of hypothesis and questions on cybernetic evolution. In *Mortal Engines* and *Cyberiad* he will work out the fictional ramifications of some of the questions raised in *The Invincible*.

The symbolism in the book is not particularly difficult or complicated, yet it is important. The two cybernetic symbols

are crucial. The Rain (miniaturization principle) comes to represent a nonrational form of artificial intelligence superior to
man's technology and capable, except in the rarest of cases, of
destroying man. Lem has not yet slipped into dystopian literature or into the dark vision he adopts later in his career, but
the tenuous balance between despair and hope is becoming increasingly wobbly, as his description of the Cloud suggests.
The city of ruins (stationary principle) acts as a prefiguration of
man's future if he were to remain on Regis III, subject to attack by the Cloud.

If the city is symbolic of the Cloud's effect on artificial intelligence, the case of the crew member named Kertelen provides an indication of what happens when the Cloud conquers
foolhardy man, rendering him totally amnesiac. Absence of order arises when the human has no memory whatever; this absence frequently shows up in Lem's work under another
guise—chaos. The Cloud is capable, then, of causing chaos
within a human being without killing him physically.

Within the realm of human technology two symbols are
noteworthy. The Cyclops is an eighty-ton, specially automated
weapon, replete with radioactive protection, an antimatter
projectile cannon, an ejector that allows it to rise above the
ground, an electronic brain, a retractable inhaustor (i.e., a tele-
scopic hand), and radio television transmitters. It represents
the most advanced military technology, reserved for extreme
circumstances, and the crew takes it as an article of faith that
powerful weapons will suffice. When the Cyclops fails, man is
forced back to reliance on his own devices.

As a symbol, the Cyclops is more than a machine, though.
The crew treats it as a warrior hero, so that in a sense it becomes a character in the novel, functioning as an Achilles or
Paris venturing out to do battle on behalf of his less courageous, less capable colleagues. The force and reality in this development become apparent in the following narrative
exposition on the Cyclops's progress against the Cloud:

A sense of gloating satisfaction ran through the group [the
crew]. It did not really matter, nor did it lessen the intensity of

their emotion, that this feeling had no rational foundation. Perhaps their pleasure stemmed from the subconscious impression that the cloud had finally met up with a worthy opponent.

With respect to the normal hallmarks for character development—detail, plausibility, complexity, depth—the Cyclops is a better-developed individual than any person in the novel except Rohan and another nonhuman force, the Cloud. Even the Cloud is treated as a character to the extent that the crew members repeatedly react to it as though it were a person capable of rational thought. Evidence of this development surfaces several times when Rohan becomes irritated with his colleagues for forgetting that the opponent is nonhuman and nonrational. The Cyclops, then, comes to represent man's technological limitations and failure.

The *Invincible,* on the other hand, symbolizes man's physical capacity for survival. The military weaponry does not survive, but man's tool for exploration does—the spaceship. Lem seems to be suggesting that the source of man's fall is his proud belief that he should/can conquer the universe (symbolized by weapons such as the Cyclops), while the source of man's heroic rise and his justifiable cause for satisfaction come from his instruments of discovery. And which of man's accomplishments is most awe inspiring? His spaceships, of course. If man is to survive in this brutal universe, it will be because he maintains his lust for intellectual inquiry. Hence, the importance of the *Invincible* and its prominence in the title of the novel.

Similarly, Lem portrays the *Invincible* in literally a positive light. As Rohan emerges from the chaotic darkness of his trek out onto Regis III, the ship's lights come on. In the fifteen lines of the tale that remain, Lem infuses the narrative with words such as "glowed," "splendor," "blaze," "majestic," and "grandeur"—positive allusions to man's potential if he but learns to concentrate on his virtue (exploration) and to forgo his "Achilles heel" (anthropomorphism and a desire for conquest). The symbolic light accentuates the positive potential.

Lem's depiction of man, in terms of character, includes the usual dominant consciousness of one individual—Rohan. Ro-

han changes in the course of his experience on Regis III, as do
Bregg and Kelvin. Several noteworthy distinctions emerge,
though. Most salient is Rohan's potential as a traditional hero.
Most of Lem's fictional protagonists (Bregg, Kelvin, Tichy,
Pirx, the unnamed narrator in *Memoirs Found in a Bathtub*)
experience fear and uncertainty, but their opponents are almost always cerebral/emotional forces: the bureaucracy;
the unknown; the insoluble puzzle; the perplexing, highly
evolved futuristic society; and one's own emotional insecurity.
Rohan stands out because of his repeated confrontations with
physical danger.

The irony is that the one character who succeeds in achiev-
ing a heroism of sorts when he survives his trek and outwits
the Cloud also presents a second striking difference in relation
to the other Lem protagonists—he wisely argues that man
should withdraw from the province of the Rain. Perhaps Lem
is able to progress in taming man's anthropomorphic lust because this time his protagonist approached genuine heroism in
the physical realm. In any case, Rohan comes out of the same
mold as Bregg and the others, but Lem adjusts the individual
specimen to offer yet another variation.

The only other character to come alive is the commander,
Horpach, a middle-aged veteran of space who, like Snow in *Solaris*, acts as a mentor for the younger protagonist. The difference here is that Horpach is a deeper, a more engaging figure
than Snow. He offers sage advice, as does Snow, about how the
younger protagonist might handle problems with which the
mentor has already grappled. However, unlike Snow, Horpach
becomes directly involved in the action, especially in the chapter called "The Conversation," where he yields some of his
power and responsibility to Rohan. In doing so he precipitates
a conflict with Rohan, who does not care to accept the new responsibility, and he reveals compelling detail about his own
quandary as ship commander.

The balance of the characters presents one more anomaly.
The cast beyond Rohan and Horpach is huge and virtually devoid of distinguishable traits. The novel contains no female
characters, and among the men the only feature that prevents

confusion is their designation by function. Usually Lem's secondary cast is filled by a limited number of flat, unimportant characters who receive minimal development but who possess one or two memorable traits. In *The Invincible* more than thirty characters cross the stage, but most receive no development beyond a name and a designation as biologist, cyberneticist, or oceanographer. Even Lauda, whose hypothesis is at the novel's thematic core, is merely an older biologist. Lem does not indicate why he leaves his secondary characters almost anonymous or why in this instance the cast is so large. One possibility is that he wanted to acknowledge how many people are in support when one man performs an outstanding deed as Rohan does.

While some differences arise within the character types at Lem's disposal, the pattern from novel to novel remains, and the technique is consistently solid, betraying little evidence of progress or disintegration in Lem's ability to develop characters.

In its literary techniques and form, *The Invincible* is a very traditional book. It also reverts to the staple topic of man's position in the universe. At the same time, though, it develops a new thematic issue more thoroughly than has been the case in the past. Within the Lem corpus, then, this book is simultaneously traditional and anomalous.

8

Futuristic Fables:

Mortal Engines and *Cyberiad*

Lem's futuristic fables combine features of both science fiction
and traditional fables. High technology and cybernetic themes
are juxtaposed with feudal settings and archaic language. The
stories mesh future and past modes in order to illuminate pre-
sent-day quandaries. The fables are collected in *Bajki robotów*
(*Mortal Engines;* 1964, 1977) and *Cyberiada* (*Cyberiad;* 1965,
1974). Some critics consider these twenty-six fables to be his
finest achievement. Franz Rottensteiner has said that *Cyberiad* is "one of the great works of wit in our time."

Their most salient features are their inventiveness and their
Aristotelian wholeness. The inventiveness shows up chiefly in
the ingenious plot and in Lem's manipulation of genre. In this
cycle Lem blends a number of Aristotelian features that tend
to surface in small clusters in other volumes. He utilizes rounded characters and incorporates plot, metaphor, serious themes,
rich tone, and inventive form. Consequently, this cycle reads
brilliantly on three levels—as playful tales for children, as plea-
surable adventure stories, and as provocative intellectual pre-
sentations on the subjects of man, society, and cybernetics.

The material in *Mortal Engines* was written just prior to
that in *Cyberiad.* The thematic and generic interrelation between the cycles is apparent upon first reading. The chief difference lies in the characterization technique. The characters
in *Mortal Engines* are mostly flat depictions of robots and machines. Lem introduces the notion of constructors in a cursory

fashion. In *Cyberiad*, though, the rogue pair of Trurl and Kla-paucius comes into its own as fleshed-out, thoroughly engaging characters. Because the two cycles are so similar, it is useful to treat them as a single unit below.

The inventiveness of plot is manifested in a number of ar-eas. Lem's ingenuity is remarkable when he raises cybernetic issues, but he is also quite good when he inverts narrative viewpoint to depict man from the perspective of robots and when he conjures solutions to the complicated, riddlelike situa-tions in which his characters become mired.

In *Mortal Engines*, the fable called "The Advisers of King Hydrops" features four ministers to "His Supreme Fishiness King Hydrops" who all curry the king's favor. Their competi-tion causes a race to see who can become smallest. Eventually Dioptricus is so successful at miniaturization that he becomes almost invisible. The miniaturization process goes wildly awry, though, when Minister Amassid deliberately traps Dioptricus in an old tin can, which is then left in the attic by an itinerant tinker. Through this tale Lem alludes to the insane dash among technology buffs toward ever more miniaturized parts, even if the cost is ludicrous self-sacrifice.

In "King Globares and the Sages," also from *Mortal En-gines*, the king summons three of his sages to astound and stim-ulate him with the strangest of tales. If they fail, they will be executed. Each makes a valiant, innovative attempt, but the first two fail. The third tells how the king's ancestor Allegoric created the world, which turned out to be infinitely sublime and stupid. Thus, in rendering the king the highest compli-ment and the worst insult possible, the sage astonishes the king and saves his own neck. This tale demonstrates man's inven-tiveness and folly, but Lem also uses it as a forum for the inter-esting aesthetic credo alluded to earlier: "Science," he says, "explains the world, but only Art can reconcile us to it." This is a theoretical explanation of what happens to numerous Lem protagonists such as Bregg, Kelvin, Rohan, and Hogarth.

In *Cyberiad*, "Trurl's Machine" features Trurl and Klapau-cius in a deadly struggle with a machine that insists two plus two equals seven. The story hints at potential problems for man as machines grow increasingly intelligent and in the process increasingly tyrannical.

"The Second Sally or the Offer of King Krool" is an inversion of "Trurl's Machine" because this time when one inventor's construction becomes an illustration of Murphy's law, Trurl and Klapaucius gain a small victory—testimony to man's flexibility in the face of adversity.

"Trurl's Electronic Bard" reveals the height of man's inventiveness and his extraordinary capacity for mischief. In this tale, Trurl constructs an electronic poet. After overcoming numerous difficulties, such as "great apes" printing out as "gray drapes," Trurl unveils the wonderful creation, only to watch it precipitate one of the zaniest snafus of all times, as it bans all living poets.

In "The Mischief of King Balerion," the boys, Trurl and Klapaucius, provide the king with the power to transform his personality and guise. Unfortunately, the politician/king abuses the creation unabashedly by playing hide-and-seek so that he will not have to rule the country. By the time the tale concludes, the evasive tactics of politicians have been rendered so grotesque that no ruler or bureaucrat could read this tale without cringing and no subject could read it without delight.

The plot in these two books adheres to Aristotelian standards more than any Lem tale except *Solaris* or the Pirx cycle. It is consistently tight and integral to the work. In fact, in this case, plot is as important as any device, because Lem uses it regularly as the conveyance for his thematic musings on man's situation in general and cybernetics in particular.

Science fiction comes into play because the setting is in the future and Lem discusses advanced technology. However, there is little detail about the technology, so that the dominant feel of the book is an "other-worldliness" that eludes location or specification. Perhaps it is best described as the place where the imagination is housed.

Lem's thematic concerns range as widely in this series as they do in any of his works. He parodies rampant bureaucracy, political oppression, man's pride, and man's infinite capacity for envy and vengeance. Lem also offers inspiring testimony to man's creativity. His chief concern, though, is cybernetics. In virtually every tale, he provides his fullest fictional sally into the subject of the interface between man and machine. More important, however, is the richness of the melody Lem composes: his range includes consciousness, machine independence, ethics, man's ingratitude, military abuse of robots, and endless unforeseen complications—to list but a few specific topics.

His method is simple but effective. He depicts man and machine existing side by side in circumstances that force interaction as diverse as any in a human community. Gradually it becomes apparent that Lem foresees man and machine existing as peers in a relationship replete with all the problems that burden a human one.

At the same time, he adamantly calls upon the wizards of communication and technology to remember that even if machines become man's equal, man may not shirk his ethical responsibilities and should not assume that the parity of man and machine collapses all distinctions between the two entities. As Michael Kandel aptly notes in the introduction to *Mortal Engines,* man is unique in his capacity for consciousness. "Consciousness," he says, "not life, is sacred to Lem."

Probably the most shocking and far-reaching implication in Lem's approach to cybernetics is his insistence that man not treat the machine as a thing. Artificial intelligence, when refined, would quite clearly be imbued with a capacity for independent thinking, action, and response to man. This point is manifested especially well in "Trurl's Machine," when the thinking machine decides that two plus two equals seven.

Several corollaries follow. With autonomous action comes the possibility that certain machines will be stronger than certain humans. As a result, machines sometimes tyrannize humans, as in "Trurl's Machine." Man, of course, is just as capable of tyranny, as we observe in "Automatthew's Friend" when Automatthew and his machine Alfred vie for honors as "Most Tyrannical Ruler."

In several stories Lem brutally indicates man's capacity for ill-begotten motives in relation to machines. Especially humor-

ous, but revolting, is Lem's "Erg the Self-inducting." Here the
machines cause the problem by humiliating a human, Erg.
They place him on display in a cage. He then spends the dura-
tion of the story plotting revenge, which consists of manipulating a machine princess who wishes to marry outside her kind—
a human. Lem's use of the universal conflict between parents
and children over marriage, this time in a cybernetic encounter, splendidly illuminates the problems involved in man's relation to machines. Here, as Kandel remarks, man reverses the
original humiliation and insists on acting as a slavemaster, a situation that cannot persist as machines gain autonomy. The
computers are no more noble than the humans here, but Lem
severely chides man for his assumption that computers are
merely mechanical lackeys to be manipulated.

Another interrelated pair of complications follows from the
slave/master mentality. As technology becomes increasingly sophisticated, man lapses into a paradox. He becomes dependent
on machines for their assistance, but he is irritatingly ungrate-
ful to them. The best example of this situation is in "Automatthew's Friend" when Automatthew and Alfred become
stranded on an island. Alfred has been very helpful in the past,
so helpful that Automatthew has become very dependent, but
when Automatthew asks his advice this time, Alfred imposes
machine logic that Automatthew does not care to hear: com-
mit suicide by the least painful means—drowning. Alfred perceives nothingness or nonexistence as a state of perfection.
Automatthew is so distraught by the advice, logical though it
be, that he treats his companion in a most unfriendly manner.
Angry that Alfred is indestructible, Automatthew spends the
remainder of his life demonstrating man's capacity for ingratitude and seeking vengeance on his poor friend.

At this juncture another of Lem's tenets emerges. The machine, Alfred, is engaging in a skill at which he is superior to
Automatthew—application of logic. But humans are not always
logical. Here the critical distinction between man and machine emerges in its most salient form in the whole cycle.
Man's consciousness will not allow him to apply logic if logic
dictates suicide or acquiescence before the existential terror of

nothingness. Automatthew wants to live, but more than life he desires to be conscious.

An extension of man's reluctance to treat machines as peers is his difficulty accepting the reality of his creations. Lem effectively conveys this cybernetic issue in "Trurl's Perfection" when an ousted tyrant, Excelsius, demands that Trurl restore his power. Trurl declines, but compromises by building him a miniature kingdom, arguing that small is not real, even though it is an exact replica, because all he did was manipulate atoms. Klapaucius disagrees, contending that humans are nothing more than rearranged atoms.

The issue here is the ethic associated with doing something just because we can and then acting as though that creation has no reality simply because we created it in a form other than a duplicate of human consciousness. Klapaucius wonders aloud, for instance, whether Excelsius's subjects suffer any less from his despotism simply because they are wee people.

When a contrite Trurl decides to fix his mistake, he and Klapaucius inadvertently discover atomic energy, raising one more concern, the unforeseen consequences of cybernetic innovation. Lem raised this issue in *Star Diaries,* too. The crucial difference is that this time he renders the point, as he does most of his other cybernetic concerns in this cycle, through character. As a result, the potency and the human element involved in cybernetics emerge in a far more powerful fashion than in the other volume, even when it applies to forms of existence other than man (i.e., machines).

The mishaps of the well-intentioned pair of constructors point to one more critical aspect of the cybernetic advances—the potential for abuse and serious, negative side effects. The most visible abuse arises in the military/political arena. In addition to the light-hearted treatment of King Balerion's hide-and-seek foolishness, Lem also raises the concern in a more serious manner in "The Computer that Fought a Dragon." Here King Poleander Partobon demands construction of a worthy foe. As his assistant attempts to comply, he accidentally creates a terrible creature called an electrosaur. When the electrosaur gets out of hand, worthy plenipotentiaries then build bigger and bigger counterfoes until it is necessary to consider antidragons. Man is sufficiently ingenious to escape this particular donnybrook, but not before the paradoxical nature of his creative power becomes apparent. The creativity carries with it a powerful potential for destruction that easily comes into play whenever pride, fear, or the desire to alleviate boredom emerge.

A serious side-effect of the technological boon is bureaucracy and paperwork run amok. Lem treats this issue humorously in the fifth and sixth "sallies" of *The Cyberiad* (that is, adventures based on the model of Sinbad). In the fifth sally, the constructors save the Steelypips from a comet by slinging paper at it. In the sixth sally they stymie Pugg the Pirate, who has a Ph.D. and a voracious appetite for knowledge, by giving him a demon machine that mires him down with a profusion of facts lacking any distinction between relevant and irrelevant. There is no hope for Pugg "since this is the harsh sentence the constructors passed upon him for his pirately assault—unless of course the tape runs out, for lack of paper." Once again, Lem's playfulness and satire sharply focus the problems that arise when a society becomes as fascinated with and dependent upon machines as twentieth-century civilization has. (Lem treated this issue at length in *Memoirs Found in a Bathtub*.)

Lem's fictional approach to cybernetics is different from that of so many science-fiction/fantasy writers. The others treat the cybernetic interface as an alien phenomenon that has little to do with our daily lives. But while Lem locates his cybernetics in a never-never world, he treats the incidents as familiar human encounters, intimately involved with the mundane problems of daily existence. Readers identify with Lem's concerns as they seldom do with alien or more abstract renditions of the topic.

Lem's interest in a range of cybernetic issues is more thoroughly worked out in the futuristic fables than in any other books. Michael Kandel has noted cybernetics is unquestionably the key to an understanding of Lem's intellectual posture. Because Lem considers Western science fiction to be bankrupt, and artists in general have not yet come up with an acceptable literary means of reconciling man to the problems associated with the man/machine interface, Lem is still struggling to devise a literary approach that will create the startlingly new perspective. New form is always the artist's source of hope, because innovative form is the vehicle for fresh insight into eternal human puzzles.

As in his treatment of plot and theme, Lem's handling of character in this cycle is more Aristotelian than usual. There are only two major characters—the inventor/constructors Trurl and Klapaucius—who, like their predecessor Ijon Tichy, are important for Lem because of their capacity to create wonderful inventions. But Tichy reacts to the problems created by other scientists; in the futuristic fables, Trurl and Klapaucius almost always invent the problem themselves. At first glance this may appear to be a minor variation. It becomes more important, though, since the constructors are more fully rounded characters than Tichy. Consequently, the reader identifies more thoroughly with them and with their difficulties.

Moreover, they, too, function as an elitist's schlemiel. They are feisty, proud, foolish, perverse cynics who mock man. They are likewise ingenious survivors and lovable rogues who evoke a bountiful measure of sympathy for man. Additionally they exhibit the charm of irresistible pixies who could easily garner fierce fan loyalty if American readers ever discover *Cyberiad.*

Trurl and Klapaucius do not change noticeably in *Cyberiad.* The major development takes place between the original cycle (in *Mortal Engines*) and *Cyberiad.* In the earlier cycle the inventors are rendered as generalized characters, often unnamed machines, while in *Cyberiad* they are particular individuals named Trurl and Klapaucius.

One other key to these characters is their dual status as sorcerers and engineers. If they were strictly professional engineers working on the cutting edge of technology, readers would quickly become impatient with their bungling. Their role as sorcerers who derive from an antiquated past adds a quixotic aura that defuses the reader's irritation when science fails. This aura develops because the sorcery calls attention to the incredible distance man has traveled in a few hundred

years. Were Trurl and Klapaucius not sorcerers as well as engineers, we would quickly cease to appreciate their flexibility
and creativity.

The final noteworthy aspect of their characters is one that
critic John Rothfork mentions—their role as slapstick comedi-
ans much like Laurel and Hardy, where the Laurel-like Trurl
causes the snafu and the Hardy-like Klapaucius has to rescue
him, after a fashion. This comic device also assists in minimiz-
ing the tragedy inherent in Lem's depiction of man's scientific,
technological, and ethical failures.

While character is more traditional and in some respects of
higher quality in this cycle than elsewhere, Lem's most noticeable artistic advance is in the arena of metaphor. As John Rothfork contends, *"The Cyberiad* may very well be one of the
seminal works creating new metaphors, identifying new concerns, and even suggesting a new genre to deal with unprecedented experiences." The force of Lem's technique lies in the
consistency with which he provides natural, recognizable concrete objects to represent each new cybernetic issue he raises.
These include the electronic bard for artistic concerns in a cybernetic age; the eight-story thinking machine for computer
tyranny; the dragon for military weaponry gone wild; Excelsius's miniature box world for the reality of man's creations; or
Trurl's Femfatulatron, the "erotifying device"—Lem's term—
designed to save the kingdom from the prince's unhappy efforts to settle upon an acceptable mate. As Rothfork suggests,
by now Lem's metaphorical technique is so strong that he
must be considered one of the outstanding writers working in
the latter half of the twentieth century.

Another apparent change in the futuristic fable cycle has to
do with Lem's narrative perspective. At times Lem has brood-
ed darkly about man's capacity to solve his problems. In the futuristic fables, though, Lem accomplishes what psychologists
suggest to persons frantic about coping with insoluble dilemmas and inalterable situations: If the person cannot alter external circumstances, he should change his own perceptions and
attitude.

Lem accomplishes this compromise through a number of

means. A subtle yet powerful device is his acceptance of the vagaries in man's nature. Lem has always been aware of the issue and has consistently ridiculed the traits. In the futuristic fables he invents fallible, inconsistent humans whom he obviously loves. In this cycle he is able to observe their flawed, erratic actions without becoming enraged by their failure to live up to his ideals.

Tone is the other noticeable manifestation of Lem's coping mechanism. He uses chiefly language and black humor to produce the tone. One major element of the linguistic charm lies in anachronisms such as "electroknights" and "cyberhorses." More pervasive, though, is an extension of the anachronisms— the hybrid between linguistic/generic conventions of the fable and the vocabulary of computer technology.

From the fable tradition Lem draws stock phrases such as "once upon a time Trurl the constructor built. . . ." He also utilizes humorous, hyperbolic inversion in addressing dignitaries: "Their Most Sublime and Radiant Constructors Trurl and Klapaucius, Delight and Terror of the Universe." There are, additionally, many features of the courtly tradition, with kings, princes, and princesses making inordinate demands on their subjects and capitulating to capricious whims; happy endings as a result of deus ex machina interventions; and suitors competing for the hands of fair maidens. Thus, science fiction thrusts the reader into a fear-inducing, unknown future, but the fable wisks him back to the comforting familiarity of a distant, ostensibly charming past.

Another element in Lem's tone is the black humor that he creates through situational hyperbole. Each situation in which Trurl and Klapaucius find themselves is rife with the potential for real-life tragedy, but Lem copes with these sources of terror and anguish by resorting to farce, high camp, and black humor. This device is especially evident in stories such as "The Mischief of King Balerion" and "The Tale of the Computer that Fought a Dragon," where Lem uses parody to make light of and thereby defuse maddening situations such as a bureaucrat's evasiveness and horrifying situations such as the escalation of the nuclear arms race.

The final element in Lem's tone develops from his playful attitude. He exhibits a delightful penchant for graphic but innovative descriptions of man and the difficulties in which he becomes embroiled. One of the funnier, illustrative scenes arises when a robot describes man:

> In the morning they wet themselves in clear water, pouring it upon their limbs as well as into their interiors, for this affords them pleasure. Afterwards, they walk to and fro in a fluid and undulating way, and they slush, and they slurp, and when anything grieves them, they palpitate, and salty water streams from their eyes, and when anything cheers them, they palpitate and hiccup, but their eyes remain relatively dry. And we call the wet palpitating weeping, and the dry—laughter.

Cyberiad combines the best features of Aristotelian and non-Aristotelian literature. In the spirit of the Aristotelian tradition, Lem employs rounded characters, fully developed thematic statements that blend with the narrative, and charming plots that contain a beginning, a middle, and an end. From the anti-Aristotelian tradition he borrows elements of the antihero, concern about existential angst, black humor, generic experimentation, and a taste for the ludicrous. Because the cycle integrates the best features of both traditions, it must be considered Lem's most outstanding work to date and, more significantly, one of the singular imaginative works of fiction in the twentieth century.

9

Inspired Bumbling:

Tales of Pirx the Pilot
and
More Tales of Pirx the Pilot

Opowiési o pilocie Pirxie (1968) appeared in the United States
in two volumes as *Tales of Pirx the Pilot* (1979) and *More Tales
of Pirx the Pilot* (1982). The collection contains ten tales about a
space pilot named Pirx who matures from cadet to commanding officer. He lives at an unspecified date in the future when
space travel has become commonplace and is alternately te-
dious and exciting.

These tales are often labeled simple and light, yet they contain both serious thematic material and the Lem trademark—
challenging intellectual investigation. The difference is that
Pirx is a thoroughly likable, ostensibly average character and
the plots are often so powerful that readers overlook Lem's
subtle allusions to his standard thematic fare—cybernetics,
chance, and man's isolation. Moreover, the books can be read
for mere pleasure, so that readers not interested in the intellectual issues are still attracted to the works. This characteristic
made *More Tales* a hit with American readers.

While the Pirx tales are set in the future, Lem so thoroughly
highlights the pedestrian quality of space travel and so deftly
humanizes his robots that science fiction is not an appropriate
label for this collection. Most science fiction depends on distancing devices that promote a sense of the alien or of otherness—wonder, fear, the unknown, the odd. Lem minimizes

the sense of otherness to such an extent that it seems necessary
to refer to a subgenre, such as space literature, in order to describe this work accurately.

Lem's plots in the Pirx stories are quite traditional, yet critical to each story. He sets them in the future, but most of them
are detective stories that, unlike *The Investigation,* provide solutions. The first few stories in *Tales of Pirx the Pilot* are philo-
sophically interesting but also a bit slow, so plot is not crucial
here. Beginning with "Terminus," though, Lem devises plots
as intriguing as any by the best mystery writers, including
Christie and Doyle.

In the early stories, Pirx is portrayed as an inexperienced,
bumbling cadet. ("Test" and "Conditioned Reflex" show him
literally being tested—particularly for psychological stability.)
In "Terminus" (1961), Pirx has already won a post as commanding officer on a decrepit spaceship bound for Mars. Eventually he discovers that the ship has been renamed because it
was involved in a terrible accident years earlier. The only sur-
vivor, a robot named Terminus, unwittingly recorded the desperate messages of the dying crew members, stranded in
separate rooms, who were trying to communicate with one another. Pirx is fascinated and terrified by what he hears. Then
he complicates matters by returning messages, thereby initiat-
ing a haunting, agonizing exchange with Terminus. This story
gains its force partly because Lem unfolds the mystery about
the accident slowly, but just as compelling is the taut drama
between Pirx and the robot. This tension arises because Pirx is
not certain whether those desperate cries for help reflect pre-
sent-day personalities housed within the computer or whether
they are strictly an inadvertent record of a distant tragedy.

In "The Hunt" (1965), Lem uses a dangerous mission to
comment on man-machine relations. Pirx sets out with a team
of military experts to capture a sophisticated computer
equipped with artificial intelligence, advanced weaponry and
a capacity for autonomous action. When Pirx and his patrol
team locate the computer, called the Setaur, an all-out battle
ensues. Pirx gets caught in the crossfire between the Setaur
and his own transporters. Pirx's worst fear becomes reality

when the transporters mistake him for the Setaur and begin firing lasers at him. Ironically, the Setaur saves Pirx, so that Lem's solution to this exciting adventure story dovetails nicely with his cybernetic theme. In the process, the solution crystallizes the potential power of man-machine relationships.

"Ananke" (1971) is one of Lem's finest stories (novella-length). Pirx is placed on a commission and charged with investigating the mysterious crash landing of the spaceship *Ariel*. The germane concern is why the ship's computer confused landing data and tried with tragic results to abort the touchdown. The inquiry is particularly urgent because the Ares, a ship with an identical computer, is scheduled to land nine days later. The story sharply draws the line between two basic approaches to computers and robots. Pirx represents the older, traditional view. He respects machines, yet he is always a bit skeptical. A contrary perspective is held by pilots who trust machines implicitly and look only for mechanical failures or sabotage as possible causes of the tragic accident. When Pirx discovers that a former commanding officer named Cornelius (who lost his command under hush-hush circumstances) was a member of the landing crew at the base station where the *Ariel* crashed, he insists on considering a human factor other than sabotage. The tension over how the commission members should handle the human factor Pirx has uncovered produces a superb story. The supporting apparatus, including thematic statement, characterization, and symbol, are extremely well integrated, as is Lem's concern with psychological pathology.

In these three tales, and several others in the collection, Lem employs one of his staple plot devices: the investigation of a past accident or difficult circumstance. Never before, though, has he so effectively devised gripping plots. The Pirx cycle shows Lem at his best as spinner of tales.

The quality of Lem's plotting affects theme. The intellectual standards remain constant. The variation arises in the complexity and the touch with which Lem delivers the substantive statement. In the Pirx stories his thematic structure is much less complex, and it is delivered with as light a touch as Lem has generated (except perhaps in *Cyberiad*).

He concentrates on four topics—cybernetics, the role of chance, the nature of space travel, and isolation. In his musing on cybernetics, he devotes most of his time to exploring in what respect man and machine differ and to what extent. The most intriguing tale on this subject is "The Inquest." Here Pirx embarks on a mission in which the object is to test human look-alike robots that utilize a nonlinear reasoning process. (The intelligence of current computers is limited because they can perform only linear reasoning functions.) The human and robot participants are paid a handsome fee on the condition that they keep the test pure by concealing their ancestry.

Almost immediately, though, the participants begin streaming into Commander Pirx's office to confess their origins or to cast suspicion on the parentage of other crew members. Through this tale Lem simultaneously observes how similar and how different the two entities are. First, he works at merging the distinctions. He indicates that in some intellectual pursuits these robots are just as intelligent as humans and in some intellectual pursuits better (such as mathematical computation). Their physical beings are so similar that they have undistinguishable blood and they ingest food for the sake of appearance (a step beyond the Phi-creatures in *Solaris*). Lem even invests them with emotions, including the lust for power.

At one point, it appears that the robots might prove themselves absolutely safe, perhaps even superior to astronauts for space missions—a provocative cybernetic prospect. In the end, though, Pirx parlays his fallibility and human decency into a winning combination and defeats a sinister robot. As Jarzębski points out, Lem introduces a paradox when he depicts a weakness being transformed into strength, yet Lem repeats this paradox many times throughout his works. Man's hardiness develops, Lem seems to be saying, from his adaptability and his capacity to trade off fallibility and decency for strength. The quality that the robots still lack, he asserts, is the ability to handle unpredictability.

In "The Inquest" (1968), Lem portrayed a sinister robot, but in "The Hunt" he reverses his approach to cybernetics: this time the robot is the quarry. Read as individual entities, these stories are mildly disturbing because of the extent to which Lem blurs the distinctions between man and machine. However, read in tandem, they become more disconcerting. In "The Inquest," the distinguishing human traits are fallibility, decency, and flexibility, decency obviously being the most noble of the three features. In "The Hunt" Lem tells of a machine that demonstates an extraordinary measure of decency. The cybernetic implications are profound. Technology may not yet have developed flexibility for the nonlinear robots. However, if machines can lust for power and perform altruistic acts as expressions of decency, no apparent insurmountable obstacles remain to block development of a human computer.

Given that Lem poses several highly provocative cybernetic scenarios, it becomes critical to ascertain his attitude toward these possibilities. Several clues are available, yet, as so often happens in a discussion of Lem's attitude, the results are mixed, making it appear that Lem is ambivalent. He seems to revel in shocking the average, relatively uninformed layman by revealing that technology has obscured the distinctions between man and robots to an amazing degree: here, it takes Pirx an excruciatingly long period of time before he discerns who is human and who a robot. In this instance Lem poses as a liberal, avant-garde scientist or intellectual who openly embraces these cybernetic developments.

At other times, Lem reveals a more conservative guise, in which he adamantly insists on emphasizing the distinctions between man and robot. This attitude is most evident in two stories—"On Patrol" and "Ananke." In these two tales, Lem addresses an issue mentioned earlier, the human predilection to place blind trust in computers and robots. "On Patrol" uses chance mechanical failure to demonstrate how costly such unquestioning trust can be; two men lose their lives. In "Ananke" Lem uses a human failing to illustrate that machines are only as safe and reliable as the men operating them.

While Lem admires man's technical ingenuity in refining computers, he is also unwilling to swallow the technological package whole. He pulls up short of unqualified enthusiasm because, ever the trenchant observer of human behavior, he perceives that there is a dark side to scientific advances. Repeatedly he draws the reader's attention to the potential for tragedy whenever man loses track of the distinctions between himself and a machine. An exchange in "Conditioned Reflex" sums up Lem's view: " 'They would *not* have saved you if you had trusted blindly in the monitors.' He paused. 'On the one hand, we have no choice but to trust in our technology. Without it we would never have set foot on the Moon. But . . . sometimes we have to pay a high price for that trust.' " [Lem's ellipses]

It may be tempting to conclude that Lem is ambivalent about cybernetic advances. This would, I think, be an inaccurate inference. Lem is able to choose a course with respect to this subject, but he is observing a circumstance that is itself invested with paradoxical, risky opportunities. In accurately reporting the mixed character of the situation, Lem must perforce indicate both problems and benefits. He is not ambivalent, nor is he superimposing a doomsday scenario. He is simply suggesting that he sees before him a situation fraught with marvellous opportunities to alleviate human suffering and drudgery and the tragic potential to reimpose suffering through other, as-yet-unrealized means.

Lem's second theme, the role of chance, is closely related to cybernetics, but with this topic he goes beyond man's role to consider universal conditions. When discussing man's nature and his responsibilities, Lem exhibits a thoroughly existential belief that individuals are capable of choosing their own courses of action responsibly. In sum, he emphasizes man's capacity for self-determination in relation to other individuals. When he contemplates man's relation to the universe, Lem's estimation of man's control over his world alters. In relation to more advanced forces and civilizations in the universe, man obtains far less control; chance, Lem contends, is a powerful force.

Thus, in numerous tales, Lem points to crucial instances where chance plays a more influential role than individual human choices. Pirx experiences this phenomenon a number of times, but Lem provides an interesting perspective on the subject in the tale entitled "On Patrol." Here, even though Pirx investigates the accidental death of two astronauts and discovers the glitch that caused the accident, he garners no fame. "Pirx remained an unknown in the world of science. Only the most assiduous readers could infer . . . that, thanks to Pirx, pilots of the future would be spared the fate of Thomas and Wilmer."

Lem's handling of chance and of Pirx's role has ramifications for the portrait of man. Lem is uneasy with grandiose statements about man's glory, so he works diligently to deflate the traditional romantic vision of man. He concedes that man is capable of a measure of heroism, but he minimizes man's potential for heroism in the traditional sense. On numerous occasions, Pirx is given the opportunity to perform a courageous or noble deed—by dint of pure chance. In sum, Lem does not cancel out man's potential for valor, but in candidly describing the universe, he feels compelled to emphasize the enormous influence exerted by random chance.

Lem's remaining two themes—the nature of space travel and isolation—are related to one another and to the other two themes discussed above. Presently we approach space travel as an exciting, challenging venture, as cause for making heroes of our astronauts. Lem forecasts a day, though, when the situation will alter radically. He anticipates space travel becoming very boring because of the astronaut's isolation and the inordinate amount of travel time. In deflating the popular image of space travel, he accomplishes two functions. First, as he diminishes our sense of awe about space travel, he again places limits on our pride about man's accomplishments. Second, he is able to focus once more on the prevalence of man's existential struggle with isolation and nothingness.

He addresses these themes most thoroughly in the first portion of *Tales of Pirx the Pilot*, especially in "Test," "Conditioned Reflex," and "On Patrol." His concern with these themes is probably the main reason the plots are slower and less compelling than the others. Through these stories, Lem investigates the psychological effects of boredom, isolation, and the terror man experiences in certain space travel circumstances.

Lem does not draw any new thematic conclusions in these stories about man's existential situation, yet he does utilize a number of symbols quite effectively to focus the reader's attention on these existential concerns. The best examples are the test flight in "Test," the "loony dip" in "Conditioned Reflex," and the three little pigs in a box ("On Patrol"). The test flight and the "loony dip" concentrate on man's capacity to handle isolation. The three little pigs in a box point to the ingenuity that individuals exhibit when they wish to circumvent the rules.

While Lem's views on these matters have not altered much over the years, his contribution in the Pirx stories is the exploration of detail. In the earlier books he sketched the broad strokes. In this collection he is setting down the detail in a fashion reminiscent of Sartre's work, using the literary forum to explore practical applications of abstract philosophical theses about man. In short, the thematic thrust of the Pirx cycle is to test philosophical tenets.

A final comment about presentation of theme: while Lem's views have remained stable, in the Pirx cycle he alters his touch. The ponderous, talky quality of some *Star Diaries* stories and of substantial sections of certain novels appears only briefly in the first tales of the initial Pirx volume, and then it disappears. It is not clear why Lem shifts away from this narrative persona, but perhaps the trait vanished when the real world impinged upon Lem's literary creations.

The balanced vibrancy of the thematic material may derive from Pirx's character, for Pirx is an unusual Lem persona. Pirx has a playful, pixie quality, his consciousness appears to be engaged with life and other individuals, and he is capable of action that leads to solutions.

The pixie in him comes through in "On Patrol" when he sneaks his three pigs in a box into the space ship and when he tweaks his nose at his instructors while still in school. There is also a pixie quality in his bumbling when he is still a cadet. He makes mistakes, but his willingness to admit errors and his expressions of awe before his missions are disarming, as when he thought, "My Gawd, I'm next, now it's my turn!"

His bumbling, however, diminishes as he matures into his responsibilities. He never entirely shakes off the mien of the schlemiel, but he does change to the extent that the author of the jacket copy for the first Pirx volume can note that Pirx "is a bumbler but an inspired one." Moreover, as Jarzębski notes, even though Pirx is a bit of a dreamer, he solves problems and puzzles "*because* of being a dreamer who is able to get away from established patterns of thought."

The mature Pirx is not a hero in the traditional sense. He is likable and worthy of the reader's respect for a number of reasons. Most importantly, his ability to act effectively distinguishes him from most other Lem protagonists. Pirx is also adept at working his weaknesses to his own advantage.

Finally, the Pirxian consciousness is palpably different. Pirx is involved in the world and interacts with other people and robots as few other Lem protagonists do. Evidence for this feature emerges when we observe the other characters in the Pirx cycle. The usual array of flat foils is present, but numerous characters emerge as real. Lem develops their background and gets inside their minds a bit, as with Savage and Challier in "Conditioned Reflex," Calder in "The Inquest," Setaur in "The Hunt," and Cornelius in "Ananke."

A curious phenomenon occurs as Pirx becomes increasingly conscious of others and gets involved with them (i.e., overcomes his isolation to a limited extent). The progression to deeper characterization arises mostly among robots, so that Setaur in "The Hunt" is one of Lem's most sympathetic "others," and Calder in "The Inquest," although sinister, is so thoroughly human that Pirx does not know until very late what his ancestry involves. Even when Calder falls from grace for reasons related to being a computer, a reader has to struggle to remind himself that this character is a robot. The reader is more likely to think of Calder's fall in terms of tragedy precipitated by a tragic flaw than as a bright flag indicating that he is a robot. In sum, Lem treats his robots as individuals.

Pirx is perhaps the only Lem character, then, who noticeably matures. Rohan and Bregg change when they accept man's limitations (an alternative that might loosely be con-

strued as maturation), but no other character learns as Pirx
does to handle more responsibility or to become more effectively involved with other people. He is, in short, one of the
only Lem characters who seems able to bridge the gap between himself and the "other."

A brief comparison of the personas in Lem's works may
highlight his major characterization techniques. First, there is
a comparison to make with Ijon Tichy (*Star Diaries, Memoirs
of a Space Traveler,* and *Futurological Congress*). Pirx is a good
C.O. and astronaut, but all in all he is still an average guy.
Tichy, on the other hand, has earned an intellectual reputation
and fame that Pirx only dreams about. Meanwhile, Pirx is con-
sistent and an eminently likable person, whereas Tichy's persona is dominated by an unpredictability that reveals him as
amiable at one moment and at the next moment as irascible,
high-handed, and vicious. Pirx knows his astronautics, yet he
exhibits little facility for theory or other branches of science.
Tichy is a scientist/philosopher through and through, interested in both the abstract and practical applications of his knowledge. Finally, Pirx is capable of significant action, whereas
Tichy is usually so mired in his philosophical reflections that he
can do very little.

The second character cluster includes the protagonists that
function as a reflector or a consciousness much like the personas in Henry James's novels. The consciousness of the majority
of Lem's protagonists is dominated by three traits: they are isolated, they seem to be in another world, and they pursue their
goals with a dogged persistence. They act, but they seldom
solve problems. For the most part they simply reconcile themselves to the difficulties they encounter. Their distance from
others and from solutions to problems leaves them outside the
mainstream of life. Examples include Kelvin, Rohan, Bregg,
Gregory, Hogarth, and the unnamed narrator in *Memoirs
Found in a Bathtub.*

The remaining character type includes Trurl and Klapaucius. Pirx exhibits a likable, playful aspect in his personality,
but he has a serious side. Trurl and Klapaucius exhibit some
negative traits such as vengefulness; however, they attract

more sympathy and a stronger reaction than Pirx does. Even though Pirx is not as lovable, Lem draws him in more detail than he does Trurl and Klapaucius. Finally, Pirx is a man of action but not a constructor, as are the rogue pair.

Lem's relation to these four types of protagonist is interesting. Despite all their differences, Lem exhibits no special preference for any type. There is also a common core of traits—isolation, wit, playfulness, irony, a taste for philosophical thought, and a sense of existential responsibility coupled with a cognizance of the randomness inherent in the universe. There is no means by which to prove the assertion, but based on Lem's attitudes in interviews and in his autobiographical writings, I suspect that each of the four types reveals a different aspect of their creator's personality.

In *Cyberiad* Lem imposed uniform excellence on the plot, characterization, thematic statement, and figurative language, evoking suggestions that *Cyberiad* may be his best work. However, in some works, his use of individual techniques supersedes the quality of that particular device in *Cyberiad*. Plot in the Pirx volumes offers more compelling drama, but his use of symbolism is also very striking. Virtually every story is deeply anchored in reality by vivid and universally accessible symbolism.

Symbols ordinarily serve one of four functions, several of which I have alluded to above. In order of ascending importance, they *reflect* abstractions rendered elsewhere in the work or *explicate* an abstraction by adding detail or by simplifying a complex thought. They *crystallize* material that is otherwise diffuse, subtle, or elusive. They *act as a catalyst* in the plot action, thereby assuming more and more meaning. Lem uses many reflective symbols, but most often his symbols crystallize material or function as catalysts. When symbols serve these two purposes, they become more integral than simple reflectors, and they tend to reverberate more richly.

In a large number of situations Lem devises symbols that can function as story titles. "Test" crystallizes the initiation process to which Pirx is subjected, while "Ananke" draws together the various human failings that led to the tragic crash of the *Ariel*. In these cases, the symbol is not just integral; it becomes essential in the strict philosophical sense. Were Lem to remove such a symbol, the story would lose its integrity.

He uses even more catalytic symbols than he does crystallization symbols. The cathode ray glitch in "On Patrol" symbolizes mechanical failure, but it also precipitates the central tragedy of the tale. Or again, the wall in "Conditioned Reflex," precipitates the accident Pirx investigates. It prompts the central existential issue because men perceive the wall as a challenge; in their foolhardy attempts to conquer it, they lose to it.

Lem is especially good when he is devising catalytic symbols for the chance occurrences that dominate man's existence (such as the flies in "Test") and for communication (the letter in "The Inquest" and Pirx's telegram in "Ananke"). The two flies, which should not have been in the spaceship and could get there only by random chance, nearly create a disaster. Both the letter and the telegram are instrumental in revealing a culprit who threatens other men.

Finally Lem is superb at creating the powerful, reverberating symbol. A good example is the message Pirx sends in the telegram in "Ananke": "THOU ART THE MAN." This symbol works as a Biblical allusion, as a sign of an individual character's fallibility and guilt, and as a universal representation of man's state. The sophisticated symbolism in the Pirx cycle allows Lem to present his philosophical and cybernetic material in a most delightful "verbal suit of clothes."

Lem has written more brilliantly than he does in the Pirx cycle, and he has been more original elsewhere on intellectual matters. The cycle has its merits nevertheless. Pirx is lovable after the fashion of Trurl and Klapaucius, and his inspired bumbling provides a winning note of guarded optimism about man's potential, despite his foibles. Moreover, with the exception of *Cyberiad*, Lem has not written a work that presents serious themes through such intriguing plots. Finally, the most effective device for rendering the intellectual material, striking in form if not original in substance, is his masterful technique with symbol. Light as the tone of Pirx cycle is, it possesses a unique charm.

10

Random Noise
or
a Letter:

His Master's Voice

Głos pana (His Master's Voice; 1968, 1983) is an intense, rich book that reveals Lem's best and worst traits as a novelist. European critics think very highly of the work; some even consider it Lem's fictional magnum opus. Lem exhibits a deftness with intellectual material, characterization, and symbolism that makes such esteem understandable. This novel is obviously the product of a mature writer approaching the apex of his cognitive powers.

At the same time, Lem's self-assurance with philosophical considerations and theoretical physics once again lures him into long abstract dissertations on the nature of the universe. When he focuses on literary concerns, he mesmerizes the reader with the charming persona of Professor Hogarth, and when he concentrates on his vision of the cosmos he proves to be an eloquent and knowledgeable spokesman for the scientific community. His renditions of theoretical physics are as lively as they have ever been. Were this book divided into two volumes, one a fictional novella of one hundred pages, and the other a theoretical treatise on man and the universe, each would most likely be labelled "brilliant." The flaw in the novel lies in the transitions between literature and theoretical mate-

rial because Lem does not glide gracefully back and forth between the two disciplines.

In its concern with communication in the universe, this
book is similar to *Solaris* and *The Invincible*. Here, the movement in Lem's thought is strikingly evident, as he indicates the
progress occurring in theoretical physics. The interest he exhibits in the role of chance also links this novel with *The Investigation* and *Chain of Chance*.

The story, set in the Nevada desert, concerns Professor Peter Hogarth's experience with a scientific project (His Master's
Voice) funded for the purpose of deciphering a signal from
outer space, possibly a message from a distant civilization.
Originally, the sound is thought to be random noise, but Doctor Ralph Loomis discovers a repetitive pattern. The project
develops into a protracted, frustrating, but illuminating investigation of interstellar communication and of man's role in
that arena.

Lem encloses the story of the Nevada test project within a
double framing device. The first frame is Thomas Warren's
editorial preface indicating that the book is the fragmentary
autobiographical notes of the late Professor Hogarth. The autobiographical notes, in turn, use Hogarth's reflections on his
own life to frame the project called "His Master's Voice"
(HMV), which contains several compelling subplots. The first is
the discovery of a pattern in the midst of random noise. With
this plot line Lem juxtaposes amusing con men with the world's
most brilliant theoretical scientists in order to highlight the serendipity involved in the early stages of any scientific frontier.

Next, Lem fosters intrigue among the scientists at HMV, as
they vie with one another in the Nevada desert, with government "spooks" who lurk everywhere, and with a separate, duplicate project called "His Master's Ghost."

Finally, within the Nevada project, Lem sets up two additional subplots. The first is the Frog Eggs Project, one of many
competing research cell groups that developed as offshoots of
the original HMV Project. Here, on the Frog Eggs Project, the
scientists believe they are on the trail of the basic creative life
force in the universe. Lem withholds precise detail about this

discovery—tantalizingly and appropriately—in order to suggest the mystery of the creation process. The other subplot,
the TX Bomb Project, is also an HMV offshoot research development. This one focuses on destructive instead of creative
forces. Here Hogarth and his cohorts, the most brilliant scientists on the project, develop the ultimate bomb. Lem uses this
subplot to interpolate his concern with man's propensity for
evil. Written in 1968, the TX bomb subplot offers an uncanny
foreshadowing of the current controversy over the neutron
bomb.

The main plot line progresses through the chaotic inception
of the HMV Project to the hope that the message can be deci-
phered. It culminates in the demise of the project as the scientists flounder with the discouraging problems that the various
teams inside HMV encounter as they attempt to work out the
ramifications of the available evidence and of their theories
about the clues they do have.

When Lem is developing plot, the story holds the reader's
interest. When he moves into theoretical matters for long
stretches, plot disappears entirely. However, even when the
plot performs its magical disappearing act, Lem develops the
discrete units so nicely that despite flaws at the transition
points, the structure causes the reader to respect Lem's
accomplishment.

This plot contains, as usual, only a modest dose of science-
fiction hardware, yet it is thoroughly imbued with science. The
plot differs from many science-fiction titles primarily on this
point. The science consists almost exclusively of theoretical
hypotheses.

The theoretical material contributes to the development of
Lem's stock thematic concerns: the state of man, the nature of
the universe, and communication. With analysis of the thematic development, it becomes obvious why so many readers
think highly of *His Master's Voice,* for in addition to the three
topics on which this chapter will concentrate, Lem raises a vast
array of other issues. This novel, written as Lem approached
age fifty, has the feel of a book intended to stand as the culmination of the author's intellectual position. It turns out that

Lem's position alters radically in the next books, but change does not affect the sense that Lem has reached an apex with *His Master's Voice*. He touches on man's capacity for heroism, versions of reality, determinism and chance, despair, multiplicity, and language. He also delves into truth, the arms race, theories on the creation of the universe, and a comparison of Christianity and Buddhism. Even a list this long fails to do justice to the thematic range of the work.

The three chief thematic concerns are interrelated, as is so often the case in the world according to Lem. Put succinctly; he reflects on the role of communication as it impinges upon these relationships—man and other humans; man and higher, nonhuman civilizations; man and the universe.

Communication between men is possible, says Lem, but it is severely hampered by a number of impediments, including the shortcomings of language and the isolation inherent in the nature of human consciousness, theses about which he has written in the past.

The most interesting twist in Lem's approach to this theme is his concern with the role of evil. He develops his idea effectively through the character of Peter Hogarth. Hogarth, a brilliant mathematician held up as a paragon within the scientific community, reveals himself in a most gracious manner to be thoroughly imbued with a streak of evil, a trait prompted by an instinct for survival. This feature of his character severely obstructs communication.

Lem employs three unusually effective plot incidents to illustrate his thesis. Hogarth notes that society accepts biographies that portray artists afflicted with flaws but will not tolerate dissipation and evil in biographies about scientists. He then indicates that he, the renowned scientist, was so evil as a child that he watched with fascination as his mother experienced an agonizing death. The horror of this incident obliterated whatever idealism he ever possessed about the individual's essential goodness and at a precociously early time in his life caused him to decide that no absolutes existed.

The second incident concerns the experiences of a character named Donald Prothero, one of Hogarth's best friends on the HMV Project, who lived through death-camp horrors with the Nazis. This scene chillingly illustrates how evil infiltrates group situations and how deeply the instinct for survival runs. When survival is at stake, Lem seems to suggest, communication becomes a low priority.

The third scene is a brief vignette that arises as the HMV project culminates. The HMV has gathered the most brilliant minds from Western science in an ostensibly altruistic attempt to communicate with a higher civilization. The result, though, symbolizes the ultimate paradox in man's nature. The scientists hoped to discover new vistas in communication. Instead, Hogarth observes, they develop devices, capable of destroying the Earth, symbolized by Prothero's deadly TX bomb: "The finest brains out of a billion beings address themselves to the task of sowing universal death, doing what they would rather not do and what they stand in opposition to, because there is no alternative for them." Lem does not elaborate on why these brilliant men have no alternatives. He simply concludes that such is man's plight—he will do evil.

Having established that evil is inherent in man, even our best, such as Peter Hogarth, Lem indicates that survival dictates several coping mechanisms. For Hogarth the two most important devices are irony and laughter. The irony manifests itself in the distance Hogarth maintains from the other characters (especially in his vaunted iconoclasm) and in his wry, skeptical wit. The laughter does not surface often, but it is most salient when he describes how he survived the horror as he watched his mother die.

Lem's approach to evil may appear obscure in relation to the topic of communication, but it is intimately interrelated. Evil, as Lem portrays it, isolates men or causes them to kill one another and to develop the potential to destroy their environment—the ultimate in disruption of communication. In other words, Lem is not considering the interruption of social niceties; he is worried about the cessation of dialogue and the destruction of life in the form we know it. And if man instinctively disrupts communication with other humans, it is not surprising that he bungles interaction with higher civilizations.

Twentieth-century humans incessantly point to their potential for communication with other life forms and pursue this goal obsessively. Lem argues that our ability in this area is limited and that we are a lower-level civilization at this point in our evolutionary process. He develops his evidence on two fronts. He points to man's limitations by showing how the promising HMV Project goes astray and ends up devising technology designed to disrupt communication. He contrasts our civilization with that of the higher forms of life by detailing how costly it must be in terms of resources and time for this civilization to beam its message over such vast temporal and spatial distances.

In human terms, the expenditure involved in beaming this message seems extravagant, but Lem uses this apparent profligacy as a source of hope. Certainly the evidence Lem accrues concerning man's relation to men and his achievement in comparison to higher civilizations is discouraging. Moreover, as he describes the universe and man's relation to it, he uses involved discussion of theoretical physics to reinforce his staple tenet: the universe is utterly indifferent to the fate of the human race.

Nevertheless, Lem is able to read man's shortcomings in relation to the higher race from two perspectives. He does not wish to encourage falsely, so he concentrates on man's disappointing failures in relation to the higher race. However, he also utilizes those shortcomings as a prod and a source of hope. His evidence develops from the HMV project. Even though the best minds in the human race are presently incapable of cracking the code, two auspicious signs emerge. Another civilization is capable of emitting signals that seem to harbor the potential for communication. Just as exciting, though, is the evidence that despite its indifference to the fate of man, the universe seems to favor life over death and chaos (as in the Frog Eggs development, which points to the potential for life).

Lem will never become a romantic because he is always so aware of the ineffable quality of the universe and of man's inherent flaws, but once again, as in *Solaris* and so many other novels, he points to a faint light, perhaps best described as a candle flickering near an open window. The only difference between this novel and the earlier ones is that Lem's sense of tenuous optimism has survived in the face of his increasing disappointment over man's bungling.

Lem's vehicle for the thematic pronouncements is Peter Hogarth, the subject of the story and its autobiographical narrator. Hogarth is the most fully rounded, intriguing character anywhere in Lem's corpus. This vitality may derive from Lem's clear identification with Hogarth, a connection to which Lem alludes explicitly: "I do not think I identified with a hero so thoroughly and without camouflage elsewhere."

Peter Hogarth is not likable in the way that Pirx, Trurl, or Klapaucius are. He is not even as capable of action as the reflective Ijon Tichy. Hogarth has other negative traits as well. He is cynical (as he so candidly admits), and he allows himself to become involved in a morally repugnant line of research. Yet it is precisely his candor and the gravity of his flaws that make him the only Lem character of heroic proportions. He possesses a classic flaw of tragedy: the source of his greatness— the dispassionate taste for challenges and for pure mathematical/scientific analysis—is also the source of his undoing. He and his colleagues cannot resist the temptation to develop ideas even when they are clearly evil.

Hogarth is a compelling figure because of these traits. Despite the fact that he shares many qualities with Lem's other "isolated consciousness" protagonists, Hogarth elicits strong reader reaction because of fundamental characteristics Aristotle cited as essential to good characterization. The reader is, for example, fascinated by the man's genius (here the charm and the intimacy of the persona are powerful) so that the reader identifies with the great man during his rise to eminence. Then later, as Hogarth fails, the reader experiences pity because he wishes to distinguish himself from Hogarth's undesirable fate.

Most striking is Hogarth's attitude toward his failure. He juxtaposes a graceful acceptance with a fierce resolution to survive. He does not rage, as Tichy and many other Lem protagonists do, against the failure of the absolute and his own ideals. In earlier novels, Lem frequently asserted that art could reconcile man to the world, but the characters themselves were not as convincing in their demonstration of the principle as they might be. A disjunction between theoretical assertion and psychological reality was always evident. With Hogarth, Lem achieves a breakthrough. This character reflects a psychologically convincing quietude that should not be mistaken for acquiescence, for, like Camus's Bernard Rieux in *The Plague*, Hogarth still searches for means by which to understand and transcend his failings.

Lem builds the quiet power in Hogarth's persona through style. He utilizes complicated syntax and long sentences to create a sense of baroque richness. The numerous parenthetical asides, appositives, and dependent clauses reflect Hogarth's skill in developing complex theories that require an ability to envision consequences long before they arrive. Despite the length and the complexity of the sentences, the prose is clear and precise—much like the mind of a mathematician.

The richness of the prose calls to mind Strether Lambert's style in Henry James's *The Ambassadors*. James's prose suggests a leisurely and reflective persona who has the time to rework his style repeatedly until it achieves precisely the nuance and the rhythm he desires. Lem's style leads to a similar persona for Hogarth. His scholarly background and his work as a theoretician on elite projects have given him the time to pursue his thoughts at length without as many interruptions as he would likely encounter in another environment. One passage from the foreword illustrates the quality of the style and the persona:

> When I came, in my reading, to the place where the subject was destruction, I expected, after the mention of my iconoclastic inclinations, further, bolder inferences, and thought that at last I had found a biographer—which did not overjoy me, because it is one thing to strip oneself, and another, entirely, to be stripped. But Yowitt, as if frightened by his own acumen, then

returned—inconsequently—to the accepted version of me as the persistent, modest genius, and even trotted out a few of the old-standby anecdotes about me.

The style contributes beautifully to the development of Hogarth's personality, but one change in his character merits attention. At the outset Hogarth proudly calls attention to his status as skeptic. He is so iconoclastic about science that he is described as unconstructive. He devises a proof to show that a particular problem cannot be solved, he soundly criticizes anthropomorphic science fiction, and he considers the Frog Eggs discovery inconsequential to the larger picture. Lem develops him as the consummate debunker of romantic illusion. Yet at the novel's close, he is accused of being a romantic. And, indeed, his change of heart is remarkable.

Hogarth concedes that the HMV Project failed to crack the code, but when he addresses the topic of the transmission as a "letter" (i.e., message), he resists going all the way with his hard-headed skepticism: "I was convinced that we had received a 'letter'." Hogarth presses the point further: "I am convinced that it was not hurled into the darkness as a stone is into water. It was conceived as a voice whose echo would return—once it was heard and understood."

At first glance, it is difficult to justify this change in Hogarth's character, especially in the light of Lem's persistent ridicule of writers who stumble into the alien contact fallacy. Perhaps Lem is withdrawing into authorial irony, trying to undermine Hogarth's credibility at the last moment, but a more feasible interpretation is available. Hogarth readily concedes man's evil, the fall of the absolute, and the insolubility of some problems, because he doesn't need idealistic, external structures to give him a sense of purpose or the resources with which to survive. Each man has his limit, though, at which point he cannot concede anything more. Hogarth has reached his limit on the issue of purpose and the potential for communication (symbolized by the letter).

Lem echoed this point in a 1979 interview. He said that he was interested in showing the "inevitable handicap of the human condition" (this would be Hogarth as the skeptic). Lem countered, though, by adding that dark as his vision is, his pessimism is "far from absolute." Radical as Hogarth's shift may appear, it is plausible when viewed in the light of this interpretation.

Lem develops other characters thoroughly, especially members of the inner circle at HMV—Donald Prothero, Saul Rappaport, Yvor Baloyne, Eugene Nye, and Tihamer Dill. He even provides integral biographical background with insightful digressions such as that on Prothero's harrowing experience during World War II and on the role Dill's father played as Hogarth's mentor. The wider circle of fleshed-out characters may result from the setting. After the demise of the HMV Project, Hogarth says that nothing has changed, that he was "never able to conquer the distance between persons" because "we are only able, imperfectly, darkly, to visualize ourselves." Lem's characterization technique seems to suggest, though, that briefly in the hothouse intimacy of an elite, important project (he calls it a "local subculture") Hogarth and his colleagues developed a camaraderie unprecedented in Lem's fictional world.

Lem's technique with symbols in this book is similar to Melville's in *Moby Dick*. In each chapter, Melville very nearly overwhelms the reader with a plethora of shipping and whaling detail, but then at the last moment he interpolates a paragraph that ties the concrete detail to an abstraction. Lem's proportion of symbolic detail is not so extreme as Melville's, but the symbolism in *His Master's Voice* is remarkably pervasive. The detail that threatens to overwhelm is concerned with physics and biology. Here Lem displays a fine talent for relaying difficult technical matters to lay readers. Frequently, though, the reader becomes tempted to ask if all the detail belongs in a novel. Eventually Lem relates it all to a number of philosophical tenets discussed above in the segment on theme.

Six symbols stand out. All six function as catalysts for the action. The most peripheral symbol is the desert location in Nevada at the former nuclear test site, a fitting symbol for HMV. It indicates the solitude necessary for outstanding intellectual work (and literally fosters the proper atmosphere), but it also suggests how easily the solitude can metamorphose into evil forms when obscured by the secrecy surrounding a top secret project.

Two symbols relate to creative and destructive forces in the universe—Frog Eggs and the TX bomb. The Frog Eggs symbolism is Lem's springboard for discussions on evolutionary biology and on how the universe began. This symbol is intellectually interesting but not especially compelling in literary terms. As symbol, the TX bomb, on the other hand, is intriguing because it ties in with the conspiracy subplot and with the thematic material on man's propensity for evil. Lem's presentation on this symbol is too complex and provocative to allow discussion here, but it merits further investigation by the reader who wants to understand Lem's philosophical perspective.

The other three symbols relate to the theme of contact and communication. His Master's Voice is the "Transmitter" that signifies the need for contact. It can also be related to a nonreligious god, much more intelligent and powerful than man. His Master's Voice is a pervasive but subtle symbol. The random noise, discovered before the repetitive pattern in the signal, represents lack of order in the indifferent universe. It is integral to the first portion of the plot, but its significance diminishes once Loomis discerns that the "letter" exists. The letter is the encoded message beamed out by the mysterious force.

Lem develops the letter symbol in rich detail. The letter in *His Master's Voice* has a resonant quality similar to the scarlet letter in Hawthorne's tale, the mountain in Mann's *Magic Mountain,* Caddy's dirty drawers in Faulkner's *Sound and the Fury,* and the green light in Fitzgerald's *The Great Gatsby.* The letter in Lem's novel becomes the focal point for most plot activity and the impetus for many thematic statements. While there is hope for a solution to the code, the letter unites the scientists; when a solution appears remote, the letter is the source of discord that destroys the inner circle. Lem also uses it to probe grand philosophical notions such as his concern for the limitations in language and the effect those limitations have on contact with other civilizations in the universe.

The symbol's pervasiveness becomes most apparent when Lem uses it to query whether the sender is benevolent or hostile. He even uses the intractability of the code in the letter as a springboard for a scene on the insolubility of some scientific problems.

The letter becomes most critical, though, when Lem associates it with hope and purpose in life, as he insists that the letter means something, that it is a message.

Quite clearly, if Lem removed the letter from *His Master's Voice,* it would not be the same novel, nor would the book be nearly so effective as a work of art.

His Master's Voice has the gravity of the great European Education novels from the nineteenth century and the early twentieth century—*The Brothers Karamazov, The Magic Mountain, Wilhelm Meister,* and *The Man Without Qualities.* The only difference is that Lem is working in a futuristic setting and is concerned with avant-garde scientific topics. Like those classic novels, *His Master's Voice* is sometimes ponderous and talky, but as James Blish implied in his comments on *Solaris* as a philosophical novel, slowness is not a defect, because Lem wants the reader "to slow down . . . and *think.*" Because of its jerky transitions between philosophy and literature, *His Master's Voice* may not prove to be a classic novel. However, the rich philosophical vision, the tragic scope of Hogarth's character, and the intricately wrought symbolism cause it to come very close to what Henry James called "The Real Thing."

11

The Book of
Ungranted Wishes:

A Perfect Vacuum

Lem says that *Doskonoła próżnia* (*A Perfect Vacuum;* 1971, 1978) is a collection of reviews of nonexistent books. The impetus for the book is the intellectual and spiritual crisis that Lem experienced beginning around 1968. He began to doubt the utility of traditional approaches to life's questions and became increasingly pessimistic. Consequently, he found himself incapable of writing any more traditional literature. When he finally broke out of the self-imposed prison, these highly innovative pieces were the result.

While satire is evident, this label does not suffice because Lem's structure is so thoroughly experimental. The book has some features of science fiction (future setting, descriptions of social structure in advanced civilizations), but what science fiction the book contains consists mainly of theories about the future, so that this label is not adequate. Even though Lem says that the book offers reviews of nonexistent books, that description fails because the book also provides parodies, satire, and outlines for stories Lem would like to write but cannot. These projects he calls "ungranted wishes." The key to the work is its search for a new genre that will allow him to write.

The book's tone is critical because the book has practically no plot or character. Lem is extremely witty and humorous in this volume, especially when he indulges in cutting, self-reflexive satire on his intellectual stance and on his own problems

with writing. He employs voluminous detail, hilarious exaggeration, and a sublime sense of the ridiculous to produce a tone
that fluctuates between wry irony and seeming desperation.
When the tone settles on wry irony, it is most enjoyable. When
it slips into the extreme tone that betrays his despair, the work
retains its wit, but it is not nearly so palatable.

Plot, such as it is in these sixteen "book reviews," is embedded in elaborate spoofs or in digressions about a person who
presents a theoretical position. One example is Lem's proof of
probability in "De Impossibilitate Vitae," in which he traces
the chance occurrences that led to the birth of Professor
Kouska. This account embodies the absurd by asserting that
Kouska's origins go back to a meteor that fell 2.5 million years
ago. Additionally, Lem parodies the *nouveau roman* (the new
novel), attitudes toward sex, James Joyce scholarship, and the
destruction of creativity. He also mocks the indifferent public
and attempts to rewrite classics. He even mocks the laws of
probability, one of his own pet topics.

Lem points out three types of review in the volume, but not
all are generic forms. The first two are parody and outlines of
books that Lem thinks ought to be written. The third group
contains pieces that invert the intellectual views Lem has held
for quite some time, particularly his skeptical optimism about
contact with other civilizations.

The most successful chapter is the terse but savagely self-
ironic review of Lem's *A Perfect Vacuum*. After an elaborate
discussion of whether a book reviewer has any creative freedom and a summary of the three types of reviews contained in
the volume, Lem launches a self-portrait that skewers him and
places him on the spit. He concedes that "there are not all that
many significant, highly promising ideas in *A Perfect Vacuum*," but he does take credit for the "displays of agility."

Then he indicates that the volume includes "an attack on
Lem's Holy of Holies—on the theory of probability . . . on which
he built and developed so many of his voluminous conceptions."

The self-parody reaches its zenith when he discusses "The
New Cosmogony" review. He admits that it is not a review at

all and asks a rhetorical question about what it is. This response follows:

> A bit heavy for a joke, loaded down as it is with such massive scientific argumentation—we know that Lem has devoured encyclopedias; shake him and out come logarithms and formulas.... If I did not know any other book of Lem's I might conclude that the thing was meant to be a gag for the benefit of some thirty initiates—that is, physicists and other relativists—in the entire world. That, however, seems unlikely. What then? I suspect, again, that there was an idea, an idea that burst upon the author—and from which he shrank. Of course he will never admit to this.

This self-immolation is funny and disarming, so when the reader knows how perceptive this writer is about his own writing, it is difficult to become upset with Lem's involved games later in the book. However, the parodistic, satiric jabs at himself are so searing, so nearly masochistic, that the reader has to wonder what deep-seated anguish Lem is masking.

Lem's final point in the first chapter provides a fairly provocative clue to the source of his crisis. He has begun to perceive the universe as a game. Once this former worshipper of science comes to doubt science, he faces a terrible dilemma. He cannot write serious fiction when he no longer has "The Faith." Just as awful is the option of writing yet another science-fiction novel about the universe as a game. These preliminaries aside, he focuses on the crux of the matter: "What then remained? For a sound mind, nothing but to keep silent." This is a fairly extreme solution for a writer. The only device he could muster to overcome the block was the "trick of the 'pseudo-review'."

The device seems to perform two functions. It creates safe layers of ironic protection between the painful topic and the writer; and it allows him to act (that is, to write) without having to take seriously what he now perceives as a game. If he plays tricks, and tells the reader that he is playing tricks, then it is not legitimate for the reader to take the book seriously or to find fault with it nearly as quickly.

This opening review sets the tone for the rest of the book. Typical of Lem's parodistic gamesmanship is the review of Patrick Hannahan's epic "Gigamesh," an elaborate takeoff on Joyce scholarship. The prose defies illuminating summary, so one example is in order. No action takes place; we simply play with word derivations: "So then, when read in reverse, 'Gigamesh' becomes 'Shemagig.' *Shema* is the ancient Hebraic injunction taken from the Pentateuch. . . . Because it is in reverse, we are dealing here with the Antigod, that is, the personification of evil. 'Gig' is of course now seen as 'Gog' (Gog and Magog)." For those readers willing to forgo traditional plot and character in order to "ride along blindly," this material is great fun. Those not ready to slow down for an afternoon of intellectual frolicking had best not stop here.

The one chapter containing a reasonably sustained thematic statement is the last one, "The New Cosmogony," in which Alfred Testa delivers a Nobel Prize acceptance speech. His chief concern is the problem of how to perceive life since the notion of the silent universe (*Silentium Universi*) has gained credence. Testa lights on a number of controversial issues in physics (such as whether the laws of nature are fixed or are in need of transformation), but he devotes most of his time to the development of the point Lem raised in the opening chapter, the Universe as a Game.

Testa elaborately details the nature of the Players, the Rules of the Game, and the consequences of the Game having been constructed as it is. The Players are the higher beings that control the universe. Two rules of the Game reveal the heretical nature of Lem's new position. As in *His Master's Voice*, he is concerned with communication between civilizations. The rules, though, create a paradox that immobilizes the participants. Rule One: lower-order civilizations cannot find the Players who are silent and invisible. Rule Two: "The Players do not approach the younger civilizations"; the Players do, however, "wish the younger civilizations well." The philosophical and artistic ramifications of this situation are critical. First, this view of the world virtually eliminates communication, thereby inverting Hogarth's assertion that His Master's Voice is a letter. Second, the Players' benevolent wish for the younger civilizations indicates that Lem does not perceive the universe as hostile. Third, the paralysis that results from the standoff makes hope an even more precious commodity than it was in earlier Lem novels. Finally, in personal terms, for the writer, the Rules of the Game render the continued creation of art extremely problematic.

The remainder of the collection does very little to present developed thematic material. A more accurate description would be that Lem raises topics on which he makes random, isolated comments. Examples: the evolutionary process (in "Die Kultur als Fehler"); consciousness and the demise of the distinction between natural and artificial ("Being Inc."); and a description of genius—the nature and fate of those who possess it ("Gruppenfuehrer Louis XVI," "Odysseus of Ithaca," and "The New Cosmogony"). Lem also touches on cybernetics, probability, silence, and man as creator. These are the stock topics refashioned into satire and parody.

A final concern is character. A narrator acting as implied author names and describes the individuals who wrote the nonexistent books—Taudlitz, Professor Kouska, Dobbs, etc. Testa even speaks for himself. However, virtually no character depth emerges with which to envision these authors or to make them real human beings.

The narrator is nameless; we learn no facts about his life. A meager amount of insight into his personality emerges as he evaluates books and reacts to ideas. Otherwise he is like the Players in Lem's Game of the Universe. We know they are present, but we cannot fathom or see them.

Other writers have used nameless implied authors to narrate their tales. Somehow, Lem's handling of the device is different. This narrator is not the simple, functional medium for the author's views. He expresses opinions, he refers to himself with the first-person singular pronoun, and he reveals shards of his personality—just enough to tantalize the reader into speculation about who he is. The most precise, albeit risky, analogy about the narrator's personality is that he inhabits his narrative world in the way a schizoid individual lives his life. He has not lost contact with reality like a schizophrenic, but he walks a fine, perilous tightrope to maintain his balance. This narrator seems to desire communication, but he wants to circumscribe how much he reveals about himself and seeks minimal direct contact with the real world. He wants to be present but not to be noticed, if notice will set him up for difficult social exchanges or criticism. He would like to be near the world but not in it. This is an unusual description of a narrator, but then the narrator in this book is not an ordinary literary figure.

Lem perceptively and poignantly crystallizes the thrust of this book, including the character of the narrator, when he remarks in the introduction that Stanislaw Lem "could not write, but regretted not writing" and so writes a book that "turns out to be a tale of what is desired but not to be had. It is a book of ungranted wishes." This is a very funny, witty book, redolent with the pain that prompted the author to create it.

12

Shipwrecked in Reality:

Futurological Congress

Kongress futurologiczny (*Futurological Congress;* published in *Bezsennosć* in 1971; 1974) is an elaborate spoof on modern man's dependence on drugs. Like *Return from the Stars, Futurological Congress* raises questions about how man will evolve if technology provides everything and eliminates pain. In this case the analogy for the betrization process is a chemically-induced, beautiful rendition of reality, an intricate deception that "saves" the individual from having to cope with the real world.

The similarities end at this point because in *Futurological Congress* Lem handles the topic in a startlingly different fashion. Hal Bregg reluctantly worked his way into the new world and tried to reconcile himself to it. Moreover, he is mildly optimistic. In *Futurological Congress,* Ijon Tichy does not conceal his disgust and rebels by spewing out bitter, mocking satire. Lem also treats his subject seriously in *Return.* While he covers some of the same material in *Futurological Congress* (spray-on clothes, etc.), he does not take seriously the idea of a society that offers all pleasure but no pain.

The tone in *Futurological Congress* is very similar to that in *A Perfect Vacuum.* In *Futurological Congress* Lem has not been reduced to silence, but Tichy howls with disillusionment and pain. The powerful but restrained grotesque element in *A Perfect Vacuum* is very nearly out of control in *Futurological Congress,* so the tone becomes excruciatingly zany.

In terms of genre, the story is a satirical presentation in a science-fiction setting, but it also involves a drug-induced hallucination that borders on a nightmare. The hallucination or nightmare, which consumes a major portion of the tale, is so realistic and chaotic that it destroys any semblance of traditional generic form.

The plot, what there is of it, is relatively simple. While attending a futurological congress, Tichy naively drinks tap water laced with an hallucinatory drug called "benignimizers." Four months of wildly funny but horrifying scenes follow, during which Tichy learns about the new world and confronts some provocative philosophical questions concerning the nature of reality. On the last page of the story he emerges from his hallucination, or at least he seems to. (Lem has so severely fragmented and distorted reality through unreliable narration devices that no reader could feel safe in making assertions about the ending.)

Neither *A Perfect Vacuum* nor *Futurological Congress* has traditional Aristotelian plot, yet the two works are quite dissimilar in their anti-Aristotelian approach. *A Perfect Vacuum* is a highly cerebral reflection of an ingenious consciousness that seldom acts in the Aristotelian sense (i.e., little movement occurs even within the realm of the intellect).

Lem thoroughly infuses *Futurological Congress* with action, but the action, for all practical purposes, has no structure. A framing device establishes a problem on Day One of the congress in the first fifteen pages; the framing device also offers a tenuous solution on Day Two (the last page). There is additionally a diary that establishes a very rough chronology. For more than 130 pages, though, the action touches down wherever the drug-zapped Tichy cares to light before it skitters off to another incident or topic. Lem's rendition of the drug experience is very realistic.

The characterization is not so thoroughly anti-Aristotelian as the plotting, but Tichy is a relatively flat character who, as a passive victim, experiences all these strange events. Despite this, Tichy retains a crusty, lively, cynical sense of identity. His character exhibits movement to the extent that his dislike for and horror concerning what he calls the "psychemized society" increases markedly. Real change (development), though, does not occur. Professor Trottelreiner and Symington are the only other distinguishable characters, but even they are quite flat.

Lem's thematic goal is to illuminate the problems that seem likely to develop when drugs are used to ease man out of pain, to eliminate internal struggle, and to reconcile the irreconcilable. He foresees excessive recourse to flight and escape, rampant conformity, and susceptibility to control by a few power-greedy individuals such as Symington, whose company will manufacture any version of reality a customer desires except the genuine article—unadorned reality. Most horrifying for Tichy, and, one assumes, for Lem, is the dependence the human seems likely to develop on the jazzed-up version of reality, thereby rendering himself virtually incapable of handling reality without drugs.

Through different drugs, Lem posits the existence of multiple versions of reality: Duetine allows an individual to develop an additional consciousness so that he can hold a conversation with himself. This society has an "up'n'at'm" drug that allows a person to see reality (to be used only in extraordinary circumstances), and it has dehallucinides to provide the illusion that there are no illusions. The combination of Tichy's hallucinations and the drugs just cited is deadly. Lem wittily complicates his rendition of reality to the point where the reader is uncertain of what is real and what is not—as in Pirandello's *Six Characters in Search of an Author* and *Henry IV*. Ultimately, though, through this elaborate game, Lem forces the reader to examine the nature of reality.

Again Lem does little systematic development of theme. His chief literary technique for establishing the theme implicitly is to combine interrelated devices—hyperbole, satire, and the grotesque. For example, Tichy goes to this congress in Costa Rica, but the Hilton Hotel where he is staying is destroyed by an LTN bomb (Love Thy Neighbor) dropped by disillusioned radicals of the 1960s. In an awful prefiguration (from 1971) of an actual historical act, Tichy encounters a revolutionary toting a "papalshooter" that he intends to utilize on the Pope. Badly hurt in the bombing, Tichy wakes up in a hospital to discover that he now inhabits the body of a very thin black woman. Several of his female nurses have no breasts. Some shock.

This shock does not compare, though, with the jolt he experiences when he discovers that his friend Trottelreiner has been given random parts of Tichy's body, a specimen that had been deemed beyond repair. In a later hallucination, he carries Trottelreiner's physical grotesquerie even further when Trottelreiner turns up with no feet (there is a cult of "defeetists"). Now Trottelreiner is hinged to a metal pedestal of some sort so that when Tichy flees his office, and he tries to pursue his errant colleague, he topples over in a ludicrous, ignominious fashion.

As was the case with *A Perfect Vacuum,* summary can offer only a feeble sense of the mood in Lem's tale. A form letter sent by a hospital specializing in body transplants indicates just how zany this book is:

Dear Patient (first name, last name)! You are presently located in our experimental state hospital. The measures taken to save your life were drastic, extremely drastic (circle one). Our finest surgeons, availing themselves of the very latest achievements of modern medicine, performed one, two, three, four, five, six, seven, eight, nine, ten operations (circle one) on you. They were forced, acting wholly in your interest, to replace certain parts of your organism.... Although it was found necessary to remove your arms, legs, spine, skull, lungs, stomach, kidneys, liver, other (circle one or more), rest assured that these mortal remains were disposed of in a manner fully in keeping with the dictates of your religion; they were, with proper ritual, interred, enbalmed, mummified, buried at sea, cremated with ashes scattered in the wind—preserved in an urn—thrown in the garbage (circle one).... We have supplemented your organism with the very best, the best, perfectly functional, adequate, the only available (circle one) organs at our disposal, and they are fully guaranteed to last a year, six months, three months, three weeks, six days (circle one).

Eventually the lists, the exaggeration, the understatement, and the bizarre occurrences culminate in a tone quite unlike any other in Lem's corpus. Lem has been zany before but never continuously for 150 pages.

In *Futurological Congress* Lem performs literary experiments different from those he dreamed up in *A Perfect Vacuum*. In the 1970s, Lem was thoroughly disillusioned; he responds to his intellectual, aesthetic despair by experimenting in the hope that new structures may provide relief. In some scenes, these experimental works are brilliant. In others, because they aim so high, they fail gloriously. Undoubtedly, much of this experimentation will repel traditional readers who still seek a good thriller with an Aristotelian plot. The innovation will simultaneously attract those readers who are "afflicted" with Lem's malady and desirous of sharing their loss of faith with a kindred spirit. Good as this formal experimentation is, it will be some time before we can objectively evaluate its worth and its success.

13

A Mystery of the Soluble Typus:

Chain of Chance

Written in 1975, *Katar* (*Chain of Chance;* 1976, 1978) is the most recent Lem title available in English. The title, *Chain of Chance,* accurately points to Lem's chief concern—the role of chance in the grand scheme of things.

Lem says that this story is a " 'rational variant' of *The Investigation.*" His reference to a novel from the late 1950s also provides an indication about the tone of this work. The topsy-turvy quality that resulted from formal experimentation is gone, as is the feverish sense of despair. In a sense, *Chain of Chance* is one of Lem's most thoroughly Aristotelian novels.

Some reviewers have marveled at the generic diversity of this tale. Compared with the genre experimentation Lem has done in recent years, this book is traditional. It makes use of conventions from the murder mystery, the detective novel, the espionage novel, the *nouveau roman,* and science fiction, so that it is not susceptible to instant pigeonholing. Nevertheless, Lem is simply drawing on existing traditions. He does not defy these traditions as he does in *The Investigation,* nor does he seek out new generic possibilities as he does in *Futurological Congress, A Perfect Vacuum,* and *Wielkość urojona* (*Imaginary Magnitude*), a work quite similar to *A Perfect Vacuum.*

The story concerns a middle-aged American astronaut named John (no last name). More than a dozen people have died in suspicious circumstances. The executor for the estate of one victim, Arthur Adams, has hired the former astronaut to investigate Adams's death. Many clues point to murder. Some cast suspicion on ordinary citizens, while others smack of international espionage and political intrigue.

The novel has three sections, based on location. The setting is at an unspecified future date in Europe—Italy and France. In the first section, the astronaut, suspecting foul play in Adams's death, retraces the man's steps during his last hours on a trip from Naples to Rome, hoping that someone will make an attempt on his life. In this section Lem initially leaves the reader in the dark about who the astronaut and Adams are and why John is tracing this man's steps from Naples to Rome.

In the second section, the astronaut goes to Paris as a last-ditch measure to consult the famous Doctor Philippe Barth about the case. Before he can reach Barth, though, he is nearly killed in a terrorist bombing incident at the Rome airport.

The third section begins when he arrives in Paris and succeeds in persuading Barth to listen to his problem. In the third section, case histories of two types are narrated. Each type constitutes a major plot line. The first type involves victims the astronaut knows about. He provides detailed case histories on the fate of a dozen individuals. The second type involves a French victim, Proque, who died under circumstances suspiciously similar to those of the other twelve victims. The astronaut, though, knows nothing about Proque's case until the French police get in touch with him. The solution to this mystery complements Lem's theories on probability.

Lem offers a plethora of clues. All of the victims in the astronaut's group are wealthy, single, non-Italian males who had traveled to Italy for a rheumatism cure in the mineral baths. They were men of regular habits who left Italy on short notice without requesting a ticket refund on unused visits to the mineral baths. None was fluent in Italian and most had allergies. As they left Italy, they seemed to be suffering from palsy and paranoia; food suddenly tasted differently. There were no diabetics among the group, and each was afflicted with varying stages of baldness, although several concealed the fact by wearing a toupee. John has been hired because he adheres to this description on virtually every point.

This plot starts slowly and builds momentum. The opening chapter is reflective and involuted. In the second chapter the narrator's hints about the case whet the reader's appetite, but after a while, interest in the case histories palls. In Chapter Three, when Lem narrates the Proque case history, the pace picks up and culminates in a good, old-fashioned thriller, replete with a conventional, Aristotelian solution.

This novel has a moderate dose of material on statistics and probability, and science is abundantly present in the discussion about the drugs involved in the mystery, but there is very little science-fiction hardware.

Like *Futurological Congress,* which concentrates on one theme (reality), *Chain of Chance* concentrates on one issue—probability. Lem raises the issue under the guise of a mystery tale, but the role of chance is clearly as important to him as the plot.

While he has written about probability in numerous instances, several changes appear in the development of the subject. In his approach Lem seems to be doing less struggling and raging. He assumes the posture of the reporter observing a situation and then relays the information to a reader.

Lem has shifted his position a bit concerning the individual's capacity to make a difference. In earlier books, the specters of probability and determinism were raised, but the protagonist always seemed, in an existential sense, to have the resources to place an imprint on his surroundings. In *Chain of Chance* Lem constructs the narrative so that John simply cannot be construed as the instrumental factor in the solution to the question of why all these men have died as they have. This is obviously a darker vision of man's situation.

In other books, Lem has concentrated heavily on the unknown that surrounds situations involving chance, as in *The Investigation,* when Gregory does not know why the corpses are moving. In *Chain of Chance* Lem is more interested in providing philosophical insight into the qualities and function of randomness.

In spite of his increased emphasis on chance, Lem does not abandon his idea that many aspects of daily existence are deeply interrelated. This point comes out when he relates the two plot lines—one about John and the other about Proque.

Another area for change, which is not directly related to the subject of chance, is Lem's increased concern for psychological matters. This topic shows up mostly in the astronaut's experience with Annabella, a young woman he saves in the bombing incident. His dreams about her arise from deep subconscious rumblings, reminiscent of those concerning Rheya in *Solaris.* Despite the power of these dreams, Lem does little to articulate conscious thoughts or statements about the astronaut's feelings.

Several thematic shifts notwithstanding, Lem retains one of the techniques at which he has been especially effective in recent years—conjuring the deeply integrated symbol. Lem includes a few "speeches" on probability, yet most of his thematic points emerge through his symbolism. In fact, all of the major symbols concentrate on various aspects of chance.

Four of the five dominant symbolic devices are catalysts for the plot and the thematic material. The two most salient ones are the case histories themselves and the astronaut's actions.

The cases on which the astronaut and the French police are working embody chance. By manipulating events in two directions, Lem repeatedly reinforces his sense of how random events are—calling attention to both similarities and differences. Chance similarities highlight the potential for murder— the men all coming for mineral bath cures, all being fairly well-to-do, all being non-Italian, etc. In short, the similiarities make the case.

On the other hand, once Lem has established the existence of a case (or in Aristotelian terms, the existence of a problem to be solved), he deepens the reader's awareness of chance by focusing on the differences or the randomness in the case. Despite the numerous similarities, the men die from different causes and by variant means. The victim named Briggs consti-

tutes a significant exception when he simply disappears, so
that they have no solid evidence he has actually died. And Proque's case ties into the grand scheme, but since he has not
been to the mineral baths, this discrepancy arouses grave
doubts about whether his case is related to the astronaut's
group. As Lem piles up detail upon detail in the case, he great-
ly intensifies the reader's feeling that chance is the dominant
element in this case and in general.

The astronaut's key actions reinforce the point being raised
through the plethora of minor, seemingly insignificant detail
in the case. When he rescues Annabella, his action relates
chance to heroism. After the fact, the newspapers laud the astronaut as a hero for saving Annabella. However, events leading up to the ostensibly heroic action thoroughly emphasize
the serendipity that allowed the astronaut to become a hero instead of a victim of the bombing.

Then when the astronaut experiences the symptoms that
the victims exhibited (paranoia, delusions, trembling, etc.) and
happens to become a factor in the solution of the case, his action illustrates Lem's thesis about the role of chance. John had
to have the presence of mind to leave a note for Barth and he
had to display sufficient calm under pressure to take the action
that saves him from suicide; otherwise the case would not have
been resolved. Nevertheless, Lem uses the other three major
symbols to suggest strongly that the astronaut was no hero.

Two of these remaining symbols act as catalysts for the plot.
The chemicals Ritalin and thiocyanates, which turn out to be
the instrumental cause of the problem, become dangerous
only because of extremely rare developments. In this case, the
victims apply hair ointment, containing Ritalin, as treatment
for baldness. As Lem notes, a massive overdose, which could
occur only in freak circumstances, would be necessary for the
Ritalin to be lethal: "In order to produce a psychotropic reaction, one would have to apply two hundred grams of the ointment daily and exceed the recommended dosage of Ritalin."
Lem uses the other symbolic object, almonds, to prevent John
from committing suicide during his hallucination. The almond
becomes a symbol of chance because John happens to buy

them and happens to mention them in his note; but he could just as easily not even have purchased them. Through the preceding four symbols, Lem deeply integrates significant detail to make a case for chance.

With his fifth symbol, he steps back to offer a grand, somewhat abstract analogy to demonstrate the capriciousness of the circumstances that allowed the astronaut to survive his harrowing experience and to participate in the solution to the case. This symbol is that of a sharpshooter aiming his rifle at a postage stamp one-half mile away, on which a fly has alighted, and hoping to hit both stamp and fly. Lem uses this symbol to render his clearest and most thorough thematic statement about the interrelation of chance and probability. The chance of a single, outstanding marksman hitting both is astronomically small. If, though, one hundred mediocre shooters fired enough rounds, eventually one of them would hit both stamp and fly—the laws of probability at work. When Lem ties this analogy to the astronaut's actions, linking him to the one hundred mediocre shooters, he radically deflates the individual's role in the larger scheme of things. His point is that without Barth, Inspector Pingaud, Saussure, Dunant, Proque, and a number of other characters, as well as a healthy dose of chance, the case would never have been solved.

This thorough reduction of man's individual significance ties in nicely with Lem's characterization technique. For a large portion of the story, Lem attributes no name to the astronaut. Late in the story he is given a first name. Even though he is a former astronaut (potential hero to us in the late twentieth century), Lem undercuts the protagonist's accomplishments as an astronaut. Then he manipulates the details of the ostensibly heroic actions so that the role of the individual is made to appear minor. Finally, and perhaps most telling, is a missing character and plot feature. The astronaut does not undergo the transformation that is a Lem trademark with characters such as Kelvin and Rohan. The astronaut becomes throughly persuaded concerning the importance of the laws of probability and chance, yet he is not an altered man for his experience. As used before, the transformation scene not only changed the characters, it had also offered two implications. It had posited that the individual makes a difference and that man's capacity for action renders heroism possible. When Lem characterizes the astronaut and shapes the plot as he does, he reveals a much darker vision of man's place in the universe. He has not eliminated man's role, but he has diminished it significantly.

Characterization depth in this novel is sound. Lem provides as many full characterizations here as he does in the most conventional novels he has written. The astronaut is the isolated consciousness, but Lem offers abundant, convincing detail that fleshes out three other important characters—Barth, the victim Proque, and a chance participant, Jerome Dunant. Lem appears to be implying through his characterization technique that the concerted group effort is more important than the action of one individual and that despite the randomness of events, there is an interrelatedness that causes circumstance to conjoin fortuitously at opportune moments.

The only female character of any consequence is Annabella. She is a significant factor in the plot, but Lem does little to develop her beyond her role as catalyst for the astronaut's heroic action and the press attempt to conjure him as a hero.

A rendition of the plot and analysis of theme, character, and symbol offer some indication of what this book is about. A few additional observations are necessary, though, in order to refine the reader's sense of this book's value. These three features point to Lem's achievement as an artist and thinker. First, he demonstrates a trait John Updike refers to as "Olympian playfulness." This appellation nicely crystallizes Lem's position in relation to his material. Like the Greek gods, he seems to be in control, involved in the outcome of events, but nevertheless aloof in a benevolent manner from the circumstances over which he presides. The playfulness comes out mostly in Lem's obvious delight in complicating the case to a point where the reader wonders how Lem will ever pull together all of the detail and then solve the case. Lem's vision may be darker, but he seems to have a better sense that he can control those dark circumstances.

The other two points are related to the Olympian playfulness. Lem's skill in working out the detail in the case is simply outstanding. He provides dozens of relevant and irrelevant considerations, yet manages to tie the whole array of facts into a neat bundle. His skill as a master storyteller is sufficient to make the book worth reading solely on the level of the mystery story.

Finally, Lem's mastery of detail provides a semblance of order that is frankly surprising, given the plethora of chance events and chaos in the story. It is difficult to pin down the source or location of this placid aura of control, but the most convincing possibility is the combination of Olympian playfulness and the brilliant mastery of story detail.

This is not one of Lem's flashier books. It does, though, demonstrate a deft craftsmanship and philsophical wisdom that render it a very satisfying aesthetic experience.

In recent years Lem has not exhibited the strong drive to produce that he did in the 1960s, but with *Chain of Chance* he offers a hint that he may have emerged whole, although altered, from the crisis of the late 1960s and the 1970s.

14

The Protean Teller of Tales:

Lem's Achievement

The reception of Lem's work has followed an interesting course. In Europe he achieved recognition as soon as his novels were published. In the intervening thirty years, he has built a remarkable reputation as popular author, serious writer, and rigorous intellectual. No living author in the United States has a comparable standing. Bellow is a serious writer who sells well, but he has not done the demanding theoretical writing that would place him in Lem's class. Robert Penn Warren has done scholarly criticism, but he does not sell the way Lem does, nor has he written a theoretical tome that would rival *Summa technologiae* or *Science Fiction and Futurology*. Perhaps the closest English-language counterparts would be Pound or Eliot.

Polish reaction to Lem's work has been mixed, depending upon the group commenting. His sales are very respectable—by 1981 between 30,000 and 105,000 copies sold for each major work of fiction. Some tales such as *Solaris* have sold many more copies. The bulk of academic criticism on Lem is by Polish scholars. His interest in Western matters and his frequent veiled criticism of Socialist practices have not hurt him with most readers, yet according to his agent he has "largely been ignored in his own country." Polish officials have, nevertheless, bestowed their most prominent literary prizes on him.

Germany and Russia have been the most enthusiastic foreign markets (first translation in 1955 and 1957 respectively). The German interest in Lem has continued unabated to the present. He is published by Suhrkamp Press, one of Germany's most prestigious houses, and his sales figures are unusually good for a foreign writer. The German academics have been the most enthusiastic about Lem's work.

The Russian following, despite official discomfort, has been very positive; several hundred thousand copies of *Solaris* were sold by 1974. Lem regularly sells out his paper quota on first editions, thereby creating a black market for his books. He has been popular with Soviet astronauts (Titov, for example) and with members of the scientific community, but the Soviet Writer's Union has ignored him.

While the French took much longer to become involved with Lem's work—first translated in 1962—the reaction has been positive. Most critiques have been brief and superficial.

The English-language reception is still in its infancy. The British, like the Americans, discovered Lem much later than their Continental counterparts. When they did, they exhibited excitement about the experimental works and boredom with the conventional books. Interestingly enough, the Americans have liked the conventional work and have been uneasy with the experimental pieces. This divergent reaction may have arisen because the more recent Lem books are closer in spirit to literary trends in Europe, where experimentation continued when American writers (and readers) for the most part lost interest in formal innovation.

The American response has been curiously mixed. Lem has been praised by Leslie Fiedler, Ursula Le Guin, Theodore Sturgeon, Theodore Solotaroff, John Updike, and Kurt Vonnegut, but as noted above, he has also been unceremoniously removed from the Science Fiction Writers of America.

The first English-language translation of a book, *Solaris*, did not appear until 1970, although the first excerpt appeared in 1962. Then, despite an ambitious adoption plan by the publisher Herder and Herder, the project fell through, and it took another three years for the next translation to appear, when Seabury Press took over the publishing plan. Between 1973 and 1977, Seabury brought out seven titles that represent the so-called golden phase of Lem's career.

In 1978, he was adopted by one of the most respected for-eign-author publishers in the United States, Helen and Kurt Wolff Books, a co-publisher with Harcourt Brace Jovanovich. Helen Wolff has brought out eight books between 1978 and 1983. Wolff's work to date means that approximately one-half of Lem's corpus is available in English, the fiction having been covered fairly well; most of the remaining fiction is early or mi-nor work.

However, in terms of the nonfiction, virtually nothing has developed. Wolff has attempted to arrange for an abridged version of *Summa technologiae,* but no volumes have ap-peared yet from a commercial publisher. The only sources of nonfiction so far have been articles or very brief book excerpts, published in scholarly journals such as *Science-Fiction Studies* or *Polish Perspectives,* outlets the average reader is not likely to locate.

American publishers have been slow to pick up on the Lem phenomenon and have yet to establish him with the general reading public as an intellectual force in theoretical fields. But his reputation has grown steadily so that publishers now per-ceive him as one of the dozen or so foreign writers capable of penetrating the American book market successfully.

Although Lem sells well in this country in paperback, his name does not prompt immediate recognition, even among science-fiction fans. Among science-fiction authors, though, he is very well known, albeit controversial. He is either lionized for his literary talent or considered anathema because of his harsh criticism of Western science fiction.

There has been solid academic reaction but no startling groundswell. Most of the English-language academic criticism covers his first five books, with the overwhelming portion of that work having been done on *Solaris.*

The major New York-based review organs such as *Library Journal, Kirkus Review,* and *Publishers Weekly* were positive about Lem from the outset, but three events brought him to the attention of American readers. First, Darko Suvin and Franz Rottensteiner included his short stories in their anthologies of foreign science fiction (1970 and 1973). These events opened the door.

Next, Theodore Solotaroff's front page *New York Times Book Review* coverage (September 29, 1976) presented the initial indication that the mainstream American literary group was aware of Lem. Solotaroff went way out on a limb on his behalf, evaluating him as "both a polymath and a virtuoso storyteller and stylist. Put them together and they add up to genius." Solotaroff also summed up his capacity for variety in subject and style: "Now mordant, now droll, now arcane, now folksy, now skeptical, now haunted, and always paradoxical." Finally, he praised his ability to create a vision: "His imagination is so powerful and pure that no matter what world he creates it is immediately convincing because of its concreteness and plenitude, the intimacy and authority with which it is occupied."

Then, in 1978, Helen Wolff persuaded the *New Yorker* to take up Lem's cause. With long, feature reviews in 1979 and 1980 by John Updike and showcase excerpts from Lem's new books (1978 and 1981), it became apparent that he had moved one step further, to acceptance by the American literary establishment.

This consideration by the *New York Times Book Review* and the *New Yorker* is especially striking because Lem has two counts against him. He is a foreign writer, and he produces science fiction. Approximately one dozen foreign-language writers receive automatic coverage by the *New York Times Book Review*, such as Grass, Böll, Borges, Fuentes, Calvino, and Frisch. None of these is a science-fiction writer. Even among American science-fiction writers, only Le Guin, Asimov, and a few others receive mainstream review response, and none has ever received front-page coverage. Thus, given the prevailing conditions in the American literary market, Lem's reception has been remarkable, even if tardy.

His academic supporters have not been numerous, but those he has have been very influential and have acted as virtual patron saints. Most notable have been Darko Suvin, prominent

editor of *Science-Fiction Studies;* Michael Kandel, a scholar as
well as Lem's brilliant English translator; and Franz Rottensteiner, an Austrian scholar and literary agent.

In terms of reception, Lem's achievement is clear. He is already well thought of in Europe, and he is gaining ground in
the United States. However, ascertaining a writer's achievement solely on the basis of reception is a tricky business, because reader taste varies from culture to culture and era to
era—often in a fickle manner. Reception also indicates only
how readers have reacted. It does not reveal whether their
conclusions are sound or why they drew them.

As is the case with most major literary figures, Lem has ex-
celled both as an artisan and as a thinker. His work as an artisan is most outstanding with respect to four technical devices:
plot, genre, tone, and symbol.

Diversity and ingenuity are the keys to plot and genre in
Lem's work. The diversity appears in many areas. Some of
Lem's books include sustained plots with conventional, Aristotelian structure, while others are radically anti-Aristotelian, as
Lem denies the reader solutions to puzzles and merrily
thumbs his nose at conventional notions of structure. Sometimes Lem is an old-fashioned spinner of intriguing tales, at
other times a philosopher explaining his positions on meaty intellectual issues concerning man and science. Unlike a Faulkner, Lem is not a storyteller who concentrates on the same
core of subject matter. Readers may question how the same
man could have written all these different books and begin
wondering if he may not have stumbled across a modern-day
Proteus. The reader encounters an elitist's schlemiel charged
with revising history, a clone murdering its inventor, corpses
that disappear, a Kafkaesque tale of a character lost in the Pentagon, a frightening foe in the form of Black Rain, playful tales
about inventor/constructors who live in a Medieval rendition
of the future, a famous scientist who grapples with evil, and a
man tortured by a drug-induced nightmare. The diversity in
plot explains in part why Lem's books appeal to so many different readers. More important, though, the diversity is a constit-
uent element of Lem's genius—his powerful imagination.

Lem's imagination surfaces primarily in the ingenuity of his plots. The mind that conjures such unusual, sometimes bizarre, situations and events is rare. As Lem pursues inventive plots, he employs numerous techniques. The most salient are his surprise endings, his masterful twists in narrative perspective, and his skill with accurate, compelling detail.

Lem's talent with genre is also remarkable. He has experimented with thirty genres and subgenres. He is also master of numerous conventional forms such as the novel, the short story, detective fiction, science fiction, and satire. Far more striking, though, is his work in fashioning new genres and in combining traditional forms. His futuristic fables and his reviews of nonexistent books offer exciting, risky attempts to break through to new structures. His generic combinations are not so unconventional formally, but when Lem juxtaposes elements of various forms, he often jars his reader into fresh perspectives on familiar subjects: *The Investigation* mixes mystery and science fiction, *Return from the Stars* integrates utopian and dystopian elements, and *Chain of Chance* incorporates a whole host of generic possibilities.

The riskiness of such generic innovation renders predictions on reception difficult, but unquestionably the writers who achieve lasting reputations have almost always been leaders with respect to generic innovation. In works such as *Solaris,* Lem has demonstrated his ability to handle conventional plotting, but a sign of his literary courage is his unwillingness to settle for comfortable acclaim as a superb conventional storyteller. Lem passes up traditional plotting in order to search for the genuinely new form. His adventurous work in genre may well contribute to an international acknowledgment that Lem is one of the few masters in twentieth-century literature.

Lem's achievement in genre leads inexorably to his strength with tone. Hallmarks of Lem's tone, similar to his work in genre, include diversity and the unexpected juxtaposition of seemingly unrelated elements. Lem is adept at creating variant tones, so that even Theodore Solotaroff's apt description of them is insufficient. Lem and his narrators have also been serious, playful, whimsical, satirical, self-critical, optimistic, realistic, romantic, acerbic, zany, desperate, sedate, long-winded, and poignant. When it comes to startling juxtapositions, Lem offers, for example, unparalleled mixes of comedy and nightmare (in *Memoirs Found in a Bathtub* and *Futurological Congress*), while *Cyberiad* juxtaposes childlike playfulness with biting wit and the blackest of humor. To accomplish these ends Lem is most likely to employ one of six devices: long lists, hyperbole, irony, bizarre occurrences, pun/neologism, and meticulous attention to telling detail.

In the use of symbol, Lem has made more dramatic progress here than in any other facet of his artisanship. Early in his career, his symbols were functional but of limited importance to the integrity of the literature. As he has matured, symbol has played an increasingly dominant role in his art. He has accumulated an impressive array of symbols, including the Cyclops, the ocean, Ananke, His Master's Voice, and the sharpshooter aiming his rifle at a postage stamp one-half mile away.

Lem's use of symbol has become noteworthy primarily because he employs it to create memorable objective correlatives and because he has enlisted symbol to enrich his intellectual statements. He can accomplish these goals only when he consistently offers symbols that function as catalysts or that crystallize the action and the characters in his literary creations.

Several other features of Lem's symbolic technique are worth mentioning. Later in his career, his symbols are more than integral; they achieve a pervasive quality and in a few outstanding instances, they become the book, as in *His Master's Voice*. He accrues detail, as Melville did in *Moby Dick*, until there comes a moment when the reader realizes that the author is seldom providing explicit intellectual statements. The reader must derive intellectual substance from his study of a complex, detail-laden network of symbols. If innovative genre is a hallmark of literary genius, so is the ability to generate symbols as pervasive and memorable as those Lem offers.

Overall Lem's characterization skill is not on a par with his ability in the areas discussed above, yet he has succeeded with his four character groups in creating noteworthy personages: Tichy, Pirx, Trurl/Klapaucius, and the consciousness types.

Lem's cast of outstanding characters is small; nevertheless, the good ones have been lively and have appeared with sufficient frequency in the various books that character cults have begun to develop, with some readers looking for the Tichy books, other for those that involve Pirx.

Lem's craftsmanship with plot, genre, tone, and symbol constitutes one element of his literary reputation. His stature as a thinker is equally important. The range in Lem's intellectual interests and themes is enormous. He is capable of integrating knowledgeable statements on topics including philosophy, theology, science, literary criticism, literary theory and history, engineering, pop culture, language, politics, and social concerns. Despite the diversity of the topics he addresses in his books, Lem's intellectual achievement may be divided into four categories: philosophy, social commentary, literary theory, and science.

His contribution as a philosophical novelist is impressive because of the range and depth of his concerns. While he writes about epistemology, reality, ethics, and theology, his favorite concern is man—man in relation to other men, the universe, and higher civilizations. He writes about communication, choice, freedom, isolation, sanity, hope, heroism, and creativity. In short, Lem devotes himself to a thorough, albeit unsystematic, working out of the usual existential concerns. As a philosophical innovator, he has made relatively few significant statements, but he is a superb "translator" who brings a marvelous flair to the philosophical novel and who renders ideas provocatively in literary guise. In this respect his work is reminiscent of Thomas Mann's—learned and interesting, although not startling.

Lem's social commentary is similar. When he focuses on social customs, bureaucracies, trends, and attitudes, he does not offer any particularly new statements, yet he is so skilled as a parodist and satirist that his contribution in this realm must be singled out for attention. He has already been compared with Swift and Voltaire, with good reason. Probably the only reason he has not achieved wide notoriety as one of the brilliant satirists in the history of this highly intellectual genre is that he has experi-

mented with so many other literary forms. His satiric social commentary is nonetheless devastating in its wit and its accuracy.

His contribution to literary theory, the third category, is a
step above that in philosophy or social commentary because
here he is not only an excellent derivative thinker but also a
very creative one. With *Science Fiction and Futurology,* he
boldly steps into the unknown: he seeks the theoretical founda-
tions of the science-fiction genre, a task few other literary
theorists have assayed—and none with the energy and the
thoroughness Lem brings to the task.

His achievement with respect to scientific thought raises
him to the pinnacle among intellectual artists. In this arena his
contribution has involved popularizing contemporary scientific knowledge about physics, astronomy, biology, and probability. Most significantly, though, he makes a genuine contribution
through his literary and nonfiction renditions of cybernetic issues. While he has not advanced the technology, he has done
what only a limited number of thinkers have accomplished: he
has explored the social, psychological, and intellectual ramifications of the man-machine interface—within the scientific
community and outside it, in fanciful books such as *Cyberiad*
and in substantial tomes including *Summa technologiae.*

In more general terms, Lem has made two other admirable
advances. He has significantly enhanced the reputation of science fiction and has helped move the genre into the mainstream. Second, he has made a serious intellectual contribution
to a humanistic perspective on future technological developments.

In sum, Lem's artistic and intellectual contributions have
been outstanding. Hence, Gerald Jonas may be correct in sin-
gling out Lem as the one science-fiction writer capable of winning the Nobel Prize. The chief reason Jonas can risk such a
statement is that Lem has the extra-artistic credentials as an intellectual to cause mainstream reviewers and literary histori-
ans to forgo their prejudice against science fiction.

Presently Lem commands greater respect in Europe than in
the United States, partly because the Europeans have always
taken science fiction more seriously than we have. More critical, though, is the fact that the Europeans have had access to

Lem's philosophical/scientific treatises—*Cybernetic Dialogues, Philosophy of Chance, Science Fiction and Futurology,* and the monumental *Summa technologiae.* Without much doubt, when English-language readers gain access to his masterpiece, *Summa technologiae,* Lem's reputation in this country will take a significant stride forward. In the meantime, Lem has established himself in Europe as a dominant figure in twentieth-century letters.

Just how significant he becomes in the United States will depend in large measure on his publisher's success in providing access to Lem's theoretical writing, so that the American reading public obtains an accurate picture of the whole intellectual corpus. The publisher is committed to bringing out *Summa,* but difficulties have arisen about obtaining a quality translation of such a long, complex book. If the publisher resolves the translation dilemma, Lem should earn from the American literary community the serious consideration that he so richly deserves.

Notes

Page	Quote	Source

Introduction

| ix | "a few fundamental ideas" | Introduction to *Mortal Engines:* xvii. |

Chapter 1

1	"High Castle"	Available in Polish as *Wyzoki Zamek* and in German as *Das hohe Schloss;* not yet available in English.
1	memories of the facts	Stanislaw Lem, *Das hohe Schloss:* 44
1	of people	Ibid., p. 58.
3	and Bruno Schulz	" '... Knowing is the Hero of My Books ... ' " [Int. by Andrej Ziembicki], *Polish Perspectives* 22, 9 (1979): 64.
3	"organically took to writing"	Ibid., p. 65.

Page	Quote	Source
4	Lvov Medical Institute	Conflicting information is circulating. Lem wrote Franz Rottensteiner that he began in 1939, but Balcerzan's Polish book on Lem cites 1940 (this date was derived from interviews with Lem).
4	such a poor mechanic	"Interview with Stanislaw Lem," *Quarber Merkur* 38 (November 1974): 20.
5	"mild brain washing"	Lem to Franz Rottensteiner, January, 1983.
6	"breathtakingly brilliant and risky"	Peter Nicholls, ed., *Encyclopedia of Science Fiction,* p. 351.
7	eleven million copies	Franz Rottensteiner to author, June 8, 1982. The figure is a conservative guess because Soviet sales records are spotty at best.
7	"Titan of East European science fiction"	Brian Ash, *Who's Who in SF,* p. 136.
7	"voice in world literature"	*Encyclopedia of Science Fiction:* 351.
7	"theme and repertoire"	Stanislaw Lem, "The Future Without a Future," [Int. by Zoran Živković], *Pacific Quarterly* (Moana) 4, 3(1979): 256.
7	Soviet-American Conference	Lem, "In Response to Professor Benford," *Science-Fiction Studies* 5 (1978): 92.

Page	*Quote*	*Source*
8	Science Fiction Writers of America	Detail on action and dates drawn from Pamela Sargent and George Zebrowski, "How It Happened: A Chronology of the Lem Affair," *Science-Fiction Studies* 4(1977): 129–43. Reference to revocation, p. 130.
8	"pretense that insoluble problems"	*Science-Fiction Studies* 1, 1(1973): 30.
8	nature of the universe	"Interview," *Quarber Merkur*, p. 23.
8	comments about the genre	All in *Science-Fiction Studies*. "Remarks Occasioned by Dr. Plank's Essay 'Quixote Mills' " 1, 2(1973): 78-83; "The Time Travel Story," 1, 3(1974): 143-54; "Todorov's Fantastic Theory of Literature" 1, 4 (1974): 227-37; and "Philip K. Dick: A Visionary Among Charlatans" 2, 1(1975): 54-67.
8	"SF is trash"	Stanislaw Lem, "Remarks Occasioned by Dr. Plank's Essay 'Quixote Mills'," p. 82.
9	February 22, 1975	Darko Suvin, "What Lem Actually Wrote," *Science-Fiction Studies* 5 (1978): 85.
9	Lem's honorary membership	For a copy of English text, see *Science-Fiction Studies* 4(1977): 127–28.
9	science-fiction community	"The Lem Affair," *Science-Fiction Studies* 4(1977): 100–02; "Stanislaw Lem and the SFWA," *Science-Fiction Studies* 4(1977): 126–44; "On the Lem Affair," *Science-Fiction Studies* 4(1977): 314–16; "The Lem Affair (Continued)," *Science-Fiction Studies* 5(1978): 84–87.

Page	Quote	Source
9	"World's Worst Writing"	For a detailed comparison of the German and English versions, see Darko Suvin, "What Lem Actually Wrote," 85–87. Title adaptation from p. 85.
10	his favorite book	Stanislaw Lem, "Promethean Fire" [Int.], *Soviet Literature*, no. 5(1968), p. 170.
10	"Polish martial law"	*New York Times Book Review*, March 20, 1983, p.7.
10	"Lunar Expedition Misery"	p. 35.
10	"autonomous robot developments"	Franz Rottensteiner to author, April 19, 1982.
11	"generations to come"	Lem, "Promethean Fire," p. 169.

Chapter 2

Page	Quote	Source
12	period of twenty years	Tichy also appears in *Sesame, Book of Robots, Lunar Nights, Invincible, Futurological Congress,* and *Official Hearing On the Spot.*
13	Swiftian tradition	Jerzy Jarzębski, "Stanislaw Lem, Rationalist and Visionary, *Science-Fiction Studies* 4(1977): 113.
13	"orgy of parodies"	Ibid., p. 112.
13	time travel	Michael Kandel, "Translator's Note," in *Star Diaries*, p. 274.
14	outright philosophy	Ibid., p. 274.

Page	*Quote*	*Source*
14	"out of circulation long ago"	Ibid., p. 223.
14	"anomaly of nature"	Ibid., p. 224.
14	"multiseminiferous species"	Ibid., p. 238.
15	"It is difficult to describe"	Ibid., p. 238.
15	"behaviorists-physicalists"	Ibid., p. 239.
16	"Tichy"	Ibid., p. 148.
16	"new perturbations"	Ibid., p. 152.
17	"not the final one"	Ibid., p. 213.
17	"dried-up sewers"	Ibid., p. 219.
18	"spilling my daddy"	Ibid., p. 234.
19	"imperial uniform"	Ibid., p. 236.
19	outlook on life	Dominique Sila, "Lems Spiele mit dem Universum," *Ueber Stanislaw Lem*, 52–67.
21	"doomed to failure"	Stanislaw Lem, *Memoirs of a Space Traveler*, p. 36.
23	"boxes on shelves"	Ibid., p. 50.
24	"let things slide"	Tom Lewis, Review of *Star Diaries*, *World Literature Today*, 51(Summer 1977), pp. 464–65.

Page	Quote	Source
26	"I started with a tone"	Stanislaw Lem, "The Profession of Science Fiction: XV: Answers to a Questionnaire," tr. Maxim and Dolores Jakubowski, *Foundation* 15 (January 1979), p. 48.

Chapter 3

Page	Quote	Source
29	"significances of the world"	Alain Robbe-Grillet, *For a New Novel,* p. 141.
29	within the same realm	See Robert Scholes, *Structural Fabulation,* p. 30.
29	invisible spirit	Stanislaw Lem, *The Investigation,* p. 20.
29	"as absolutely inhuman"	Ibid., p. 40.
30	"no final solutions"	Stanislaw Lem, *Summa technologiae,* p. 400.
30	"Gregory began to feel"	*Investigation,* p. 50.
31	reflect those values	Stanley Fogel, "The Investigation: Stanislaw Lem's Pynchonesque Novel," *Riverside Quarterly* 6(1977): 287.
32	criminal perpetrator exists	Lem, *Investigation,* exists p. 161.
33	"Actually I'm more on the defensive"	Ibid., p. 139.
34	"kind of posthumous order"	Ibid., p. 136.

Page	*Quote*	*Source*
35	"pyramids of chaos"	Ibid., p. 179.
36	"fossilized traditionalists"	Stanislaw Lem, "Philip K. Dick: A Visionary Among the Charlatans," p. 61.

Chapter 4

41	"cornerstone of this world"	Stanislaw Lem, *Return from the Stars,* p. 207.
42	"old, old, old"	George R. R. Martin, *Book World,* June 22, 1980, p. 7.
42	"look courtly"	John Updike, *New Yorker,* September 8, 1980, p. 110.
42	"unbetrizated present"	Ibid.
43	"you were afraid"	Lem, *Return,* p. 197.
43	"I had taken advantage"	Ibid., pp. 198–99.
44	"continuing consciousness"	Ibid., p. 212.
45	"I don't know"	Ibid., p. 227.
45	"O wretched one"	Ibid., p. 212.
48	one of his better books	Lem, *Pacific Quarterly* interview, p. 256. "I feel *Return from the Stars* to be a rather poor work."

Page	Quote	Source

Chapter 5

50	"Rheya"	In Polish the name is "Harey." Since no English counterpart exists, it makes no sense to change the name in the English translation, although Kilmartin and Cox, the translators, did so.
50	"autometamor-phosis"	Stanislaw Lem, *Solaris*, p. 24.
51	*"Solaris"*	Lem, *Pacific Quarterly* interview, p. 258.
51	"This is a gnosseological drama"	Ibid., p. 259.
52	"The age-old faith"	Lem, *Solaris*, p. 204.
52	"time of cruel miracles was not past"	Ibid.
53	higher level of existence	Darko Suvin, "Three World Paradigms for SF: Asimov, Yefremov, Lem," *Pacific Quarterly* 4, 3(1979): 276.
53	anthropomorphism ought to be limited	Lem, *Pacific Quarterly* interview, p. 259.
53	infinite nature	Suvin, pp. 279–80.
54	"aware of his powerlessness"	*Solaris*, p. 198.

Page	Quote	Source
54	"a god who simply is"	Ibid., p. 199.
54	creation of man	Ibid., p. 198.
55	Ketterer and Geier	David Ketterer, "*Solaris* and the Illegitimate Suns of Science Fiction," *Extrapolation* 14(1972): 73–89; Manfred Geier, "Stanislaw Lems Phantastischer Ozean," *Ueber Stanislaw Lem*, pp. 96–163.
56	mirrors, glass, and doors	Ketterer: 80.
56	critically acclaimed authors anywhere	Ibid., p. 75.
57	female sexuality	Ketterer's thesis; see pp. 84–87.
57	Ketterer and Geier suggest	Ketterer, p. 87 and Geier, pp. 150–52. Much of Geier's monograph is devoted to this assertion.
57	"programmed mind"	Lem, *Pacific Quarterly* interview, p. 258.
59	"its sway"	David L. Lavery, " 'The Genius of the Sea': Wallace Stevens' 'The Idea of Order at Key West,' Stanislaw Lem's *Solaris,* and the Earth as a Muse," *Extrapolation* 21(1980): 105.
59	"within its textures"	Ibid., p. 102.
60	"being invaded through and through"	Lem, *Solaris,* p. 180.

Page	Quote	Source

Chapter 6

63	"the Great Collapse"	Stanislaw Lem, *Memoirs Found in a Bathtub*, p. 1.
63	"Kap-Eh-Taahl"	Ibid., p. 10.
64	"hermetic isolation"	Ibid., p. 10.
65	"extremely hazardous"	Ibid., p. 18.
65	"It's difficult, complicated"	Ibid., p. 25.
65	"I was beginning to doubt"	Ibid., p. 58.
66	" 'But you have no appointment' "	Ibid., pp. 81–82.
67	"Hey, the Building, hey!"	Ibid., p. 157.

Chapter 7

70	mystery novel	Ursula Le Guin, "European SF," *Science-Fiction Studies* 1, 3 (1974): 183.
70	" 'stay on this planet' "	Stanislaw Lem, *The Invincible*, p. 104.
73	"solid and central"	Le Guin, p. 183.
74	"How foolhardy, how ludicrous"	Lem, *The Invincible*, p. 142.

Page	*Quote*	*Source*
75	for Lem's protagonists	Jerzy Jarzębski, 115. Jarzębski cites Maciej Szybist as his source: "His Master's Voice From the Radio," *Życie Literackie* 26 (1969).
75	"bottom of the valley"	Lem, *The Invincible*, p. 177.
75	"gigantic human figure"	Ibid.
75	"shadow in the clouds"	*Foundation* interview, p. 43.
76	"science explains the world"	Lem, *Mortal Engines*, p. 113.
76	"as if it were indeed invincible"	Lem, *The Invincible*, p. 183.
76	"undefinable formations"	Ibid., p. 31.
78	"A sense of gloating satisfaction"	Ibid., p. 126.

Chapter 8

| 82 | *Cyberiad;* 1965, 1977 | The publishing history of the fables is complicated. The eleven fables collected in *Mortal Engines* were originally part of the Polish volume entitled *Bajki robotów (Fables for Robots;* 1964). Most but not all of the *Bajki robotów* fables were added to the 1967 edition of *Cyberiada*. The 1972 edition of *Cyberiada* includes all eleven fables that Kandel collected in |

Page	Quote	Source
		Mortal Engines. For details on the history, see Franz Rottensteiner's bibliography in *Quarber Merkur* no. 38 (1974): 70–71.
		The *Mortal Engines* collection, however, contains other material, including "Dr. Vliperdius" from the Polish edition of *Star Diaries* (not in the American edition), "The Hunt" from *More Tales of Pirx the Pilot,* and *The Mask,* published in Poland in a volume entitled *Maska.*
82	twenty-six fables	Eleven in *Mortal Engines;* fifteen in *Cyberiad.*
82	"in our time"	Franz Rottensteiner, "Stanislaw Lem: A Profile," *Luna Monthly* 31(December 1971), p. 8.
83	"Science explains the world"	Stanislaw Lem, *Mortal Engines,* p. 113.
84	"gray drapes"	Stanislaw Lem, *Cyberiad,* p. 45.
85	"sacred to Lem"	Lem, *Mortal Engines,* p. xx.
86	slavemaster	Michael Kandel, "Stanislaw Lem on Men and Robots," *Extrapolation* 14(1972): 17.
88	model of Sinbad	*Foundation* interview, p. 43.
88	"for lack of paper"	Lem, *Cyberiad,* p. 160.
88	intellectual posture	Kandel, *Extrapolation,* p. 14.
89	sorcerers and engineers	Jerzy Jarzębski's terms, p. 123.

Page	Quote	Source
90	after a fashion	John Rothfork, "Cybernetics and a Humanistic Fiction: Stanislaw Lem's *The Cyberiad,*" *Research Studies* 45, 3(1977): 125.
90	"unprecedented experiences"	Ibid., p. 126.
90	"erotifying device"	Lem, *Cyberiad,* p. 108.
91	"cyberhorses"	Jarzębski, p. 121.
91	"the constructor built"	Lem, *Cyberiad,* p. 9.
91	"Terror of the Universe"	Ibid., p. 80.
92	"In the morning they wet themselves"	Ibid., p. 290.

Chapter 9

93	tedious and exciting	Pirx also appears in *Invasion from Aldebaran, Book of Robots, Lunar Night, The Hunt,* and *Bezsenność.*
96	transformed into strength	Jarzębski, p. 121.
98	" 'high price for that trust' "	Stanislaw Lem, *Tales of Pirx the Pilot,* p. 112.
99	"fate of Thomas and Wilmer"	Ibid., p. 139.
100	"My Gawd, I'm next"	Ibid., p. 14.

Page	Quote	Source
101	"established patterns of thought"	Jarzębski, p. 120.
104	"verbal suit of clothes"	Stanislaw Lem, *His Master's Voice*, p. 47.

Chapter 10

109	"no alternative for them"	Stanislaw Lem, *His Master's Voice*, p. 194.
111	"without camouflage elsewhere"	*New York Times Book Review*, March 20, 1983, p. 35.
112	"When I came"	Ibid., pp. 3–4.
113	"we had received a 'letter' "	Ibid., p. 192.
113	"heard and understood"	Ibid., p. 195.
113	"handicap of the human condition"	*Foundation* interview, p. 48.
114	"far from absolute"	Ibid., p. 48.
114	"to visualize ourselves"	*His Master's Voice*, pp. 198–99.
114	"a local subculture"	Ibid., p. 67.
116	"to slow down . . . and *think*"	James Blish, *Magazine of Fantasy and Science Fiction* 40(1971): 43.

Chapter 11

117	"ungranted wishes"	Stanislaw Lem, *A Perfect Vacuum*, p. 8.

Page	Quote	Source
118	"ideas in *A Perfect Vacuum*"	Ibid., p. 5.
118	"displays of agility"	Ibid.
118	"so many of his voluminous conceptions"	Ibid., p. 6.
119	"A bit heavy for a joke"	Ibid.
119	"to keep silent"	Ibid., p. 7.
119	"trick of the 'pseudo-review' "	Ibid.
120	"(Gog and Magog)"	Ibid., p. 32.
120	"The Players do not approach"	Ibid., p. 221.
120	"wish the younger civilizations well"	Ibid., p. 222.
122	"regretted not writing"	Ibid., p. 5.
122	"book of ungranted wishes"	Ibid., p. 8.

Chapter 12

124	"psychemized society"	Stanislaw Lem, *Futurological Congress,* p. 67.
126	"Dear Patient"	Ibid., pp. 49–50.

Chapter 13

128	"a rational variant"	*Foundation* interview, p. 42.

Page	Quote	Source
132	"recommended dosage of Ritalin"	Stanislaw Lem, *Chain of Chance*, p. 171.
134	"Olympian playfulness"	John Updike, *New Yorker*, February 26, 1979, p. 116.

Chapter 14

Page	Quote	Source
136	each major work of fiction	Franz Rottensteiner and Klaus Staemmler, "Stanislaw-Lem-Bibliographie," *Ueber Stanislaw Lem*, ed. Werner Berthel (Frankfurt: Suhrkamp, 1981), pp. 222–32.
136	"ignored in his own country"	Franz Rottensteiner to author, June 8, 1982.
137	sold by 1974	"Stanislaw Lem Bibliographie," *Quarber Merkur:* 81.
137	black market for his books	J. M. Purcell, "Tarkovsky's Film *Solaris* (1972): A Freudian Slip?", *Extrapolation* 19(1978): 131.
137	Herder and Herder	Rottensteiner, *Luna Monthly*, p. 22.
139	"with which it is occupied"	All three quotations from Theodore Solotaroff, *New York Times Book Review*, September 29, 1976, p. 1.
139	(1978 and 1981)	*New Yorker*, July 24, 1978, pp. 26–42; September 18, 1978, pp. 36–44; December 11, 1978, pp. 38–54; October 12, 1981, pp. 42–48; November 2, 1981, pp. 48–53; November 30, 1981, pp. 44–53; December 21, 1981, pp. 45–50.

Bibliography

I. Works by Lem

A. Books (by Polish publication date)

Man from Mars. Not translated. *Człowiek z Marsa.* Katowicz in *Co Tydzien Powiesc,* 1946. Science-fiction novel.

Astronauts. Not translated. *Astronauci.* Warsaw: Czytelnik, 1951. Science-fiction novel about an expedition to Venus. Lem is already exhibiting concern about how man will use his technology.

Sesame. Not translated. *Sezam i inne opowiadania.* Warsaw: Iskry, 1954. Story collection—includes early Tichy tales.

The Magellan Nebula. Not translated. *Obłok Magellana.* Warsaw: Iskry, 1955. Science-fiction novel about life on the spaceship *Gaea.*

Time Not Lost. Not translated. *Czas nieutracony.* Cracow: Wydawnictwo Literackie, 1955. Nonscience-fiction trilogy. About an isolated intellectual who searches for his place in society.

Cybernetic Dialogues. Not translated. *Dialogi.* Cracow: Wydawnictwo Literackie, 1957. Modeled on the Berkleyan dialogues. Imposes a cybernetic view on sociology, human consciousness, and language.

Star Diaries. Tr. Michael Kandel. New York: Seabury Press, 1976; *Dzienniki gwiazdowe.* Warsaw: Iskry, 1957.

Eden. Not translated. *Eden.* Warsaw: Iskry, 1959. Science-fiction novel about humans on an alien planet. An early rendition of Lem's concern about evolution and the problems involved when people try to control the evolutionary process.

Invasion from Aldebaran. Not translated. *Inwazja z Aldebarana.* Cracow: Wydawnictwo Literackie, 1959. Story collection. Some stories that have not been translated; the first Pirx tales, which have been translated.

The Investigation. Tr. Adele Milch. New York: Seabury Press, 1974; *Sledztwo.* Warsaw: Wydawnictwo Ministerstwa Obrony Narodowej, 1959.

The Book of the Robots. Not translated. *Księga robotów.* Warsaw: Iskry, 1961. Story collection. The first Tichy; more Pirx; an untranslated tale.

Memoirs Found in a Bathtub. Tr. Michael Kandel and Christine Rose. New York: Seabury Press, 1973; *Pamiętnik znaleziony w wannie.* Cracow: Wydawnictwo Literackie, 1961.

Return from the Stars. Tr. Barbara Marszal and Frank Simpson. New York: Helen and Kurt Wolff Books/Harcourt Brace Jovanovich, 1980; *Powrót z gwiazd.* Warsaw: Czytelnik, 1961.

Solaris. Tr. from French by Joanna Kilmartin and Steve Cox. New York: Walker and Co., 1970; *Solaris.* Warsaw: Wydawnictwo Ministerstwa Obrony Narodowej, 1961.

Getting into Orbit. Not translated. *Wejście na orbite.* Cracow: Wydawnictwo Literackie, 1962. Essays on fiction, futurology, and technology.

Lunar Night. Not translated. *Noc księżycowa.* Cracow: Wydawnictwo Literackie, 1963. Story collection and four TV plays. More Tichy; more Pirx; Professor Tarantoga; other material.

Bajki robotów. Cracow: Wydawnictwo Literackie, 1964. See *Mortal Engines* for detail.

The Invincible. Tr. from German by Wendayne Ackerman. New York: Seabury Press, 1973; *Niezwyciężony i inne opowiadania.* Warsaw: Wydawnictwo Ministerstwa Obrony Narodowej, 1964. The Polish edition contains additional stories.

Summa technologiae. Not translated. *Summa technologiae.* Cracow: Wydawnictwo Literackie, 1964. Long philosophical treatise (600 pages) on specific topics, such as cybernetics and biological engineering; also contains pronouncements on general issues, such as reason, biology, and the nature of consciousness.

Cyberiad. Tr. Michael Kandel. New York: Seabury Press, 1974; *Cyberiada.* Cracow: Wydawnictwo Literackie, 1965.

Polowanie. Cracow: Wydawnictwo Literackie, 1965. See *Mortal Engines* for detail. Includes three new Pirx, one Trurl and Klapaucius, and a nonseries story.

Let Us Save the Universe and Other Stories. Not translated. *Ratujumy kosmos i inne opowiadania.* Cracow: Wydawnictwo Literackie, 1966. Story collection. Repeats on Pirx and Tichy.

High Castle. Not translated. *Wysoki Zamek.* Warsaw: Wydawnictwo Ministerstwo Obrony Narodowej, 1966. Anecdotal, analytical autobiography (very loose on chronology). Covers the early years.

His Master's Voice. Tr. Michael Kandel. New York: Helen and Kurt Wolff Books/Harcourt Brace Jovanovich, 1983; *Głos pana.* Warsaw: Czytelnik, 1968.

Philosophy of Chance. Not translated. *Filozofia przypadku.* Cracow: Wydawnictwo Literackie, 1968. A theoretical attempt to counter the abstractness of Roman Ingarden's phenomenological school of literature—with an empirical theory. As long as *Summa technologiae.* Two sections. 1. General level establishes hypotheses and rules. 2. Practical application of general theory (on various literary works). Lem seeks to establish the verifiable value in particular works of art.

Tales of Pirx the Pilot. Tr. Louis Iribarne. New York: Helen and Kurt Wolff Books/Harcourt Brace Jovanovich, 1979; *Opowiesci o pilocie Pirxie.* Cracow: Wydawnictwo Literackie, 1968. Contains "The Test," "On Patrol," "The Albatross" (1959; originally in *Invasion from Aldebaran*), "Terminus" (1961; originally in *The Book of the Robots*), and "Conditioned Reflex" (1963; originally in *Lunar Night*).

Stories. Not Translated. *Opowiadania.* Cracow: Wydawnictwo Literackie, 1969. Story collection. All repeats.

Science Fiction and Futurology. Not translated. *Fantastyka i futurologia.* Cracow: Wydawnictwo Literackie, 1970. An attempt to generate an empirical theory for the science-fiction genre. Two volumes (total nearly 1200 pages).

Futurological Congress. Tr. Michael Kandel. New York: Seabury Press, 1974; *Bezsenność.* Cracow: Wydawnictwo Literackie, 1971. The American edition contains only Part One of Bezsenność. "Non Serviam" is in the American edition of *A Perfect Vacuum,* and "Ananke" is in *More Tales of Pirx the Pilot.*

A Perfect Vacuum. Tr. Michael Kandel. New York: Helen and Kurt Wolff Books/Harcourt Brace Jovanovich, 1978; *Doskonala próżnia.* Warsaw: Czytelnik, 1971. American edition contains "Non Serviam" from Bezsenność.

Imaginary Magnitude. Tr. Marc Heine. New York: Helen and Kurt Wolff Books/Harcourt Brace Jovanovich, forthcoming; *Wielkosć urojona.* Warsaw: Czytelnik, 1973. An experiment in form, this time with introductions to nonexistent books.

Selected Stories. Not translated. *Opowiadania wybrane.* Cracow: Wydawnictwo Literackie, 1973. Story collection featuring repeats on Tichy, Pirx, and Trurl and Klapaucius; *The Hunt;* and *The Invincible.*

Essays and Sketches. Not translated. *Rozprawy i szkice.* Cracow: Wydawnictwo Literackie, 1975. On literature, science fiction, and science.

Chain of Chance. Tr. Louis Iribarne. New York: Helen and Kurt Wolff Books/Harcourt Brace Jovanovich, 1978; *Katar.* Cracow: Wydawnictwo Literackie, 1976. [Also referred to as *Running Nose.*]

Maska. Cracow: Wydawnictwo Literackie, 1976. See *Mortal Engines* for detail. Includes "The Mask," a new Tichy memoir, a new Trurl and Klapaucius story, and reprints of three TV plays from *Lunar Night.*

Suplement. Not translated. Cracow: Wydawnictwo Literackie, 1976. Story collection. Three Tichy, one *Cyberiad,* and one Pirx.

Mortal Engines. Tr. Michael Kandel. New York: Seabury Press, 1977. Contains material from four Polish volumes. 1. *Bajki robotów (Fables for Robots)* in *Cyberiada,* 3rd ed. Cracow: Wydawnictwo Literackie, 1972; 2. *Polowanie (The Hunt).* Cracow: Wydawnictwo Literackie, 1965; 3. *Maska (The Mask).* Cracow: Wydawnictwo Literackie, 1976; 4; "The Sanatorium of Dr. Vliperdius" in *Dzienniki gwaizdowe,* 4th ed. Warsaw: Czytelnik, 1971.

The Repetition. Not translated. *Powtórka.* Warsaw: Iskry, 1979. Contains "Powtórka," "Godzina przyjec professor Tarontogi," and "Noc księżyćowa." A new Trurl and Klapaucius, a Professor Tarantoga play, and a radio script.

Golem XIV. Not translated. Cracow: Wydawnictwo Literackie, 1981. The "Golem" speech from *Imaginary Magnitude,* a new speech, and an Afterword.

Memoirs of a Space Traveler: Further Reminiscences of Ijon Tichy. Tr. Joel Stern and Maria Swiecka-Ziemianek. New York: Helen and Kurt Wolff Books/Harcourt Brace Jovanovich, 1981. Contains remaining tales from *Dzienniki gwiazdowe (Star Diaries).*

The Cosmic Carnival of Stanislaw Lem. Ed. Michael Kandel. New York: Continuum Publishing, 1981. An anthology. Contains "The Test" from *Tales of Pirx the Pilot;* "Les Robinsonades" from *A Per-*

fect Vacuum; four futuristic fables; and excerpts from *Return from the Stars, Solaris, The Invincible,* and *Futurological Congress.*
More Tales of Pirx the Pilot. Tr. Michael Kandel and Louis Iribarne with the assistance of Magdalena Majcherczyk. New York: Helen and Kurt Wolff Books/Harcourt Brace Jovanovich, 1982. Contains "Pirx's Tale," "The Accident," "The Hunt" (1965 in *Polowanie*); "The Inquest" (1968 in *Opowieści o pilocie Pirxie*); and "Ananke" (1971 in *Bezsenność*).
Official Hearing On the Spot. Not translated. *Wizja Lokalna.* Cracow: Wydawnictwo Literackie, 1982. Tichy tale with a new twist on evolution.

B. Books (by American publication date)

Solaris, 1970.
The Invincible, 1973.
Memoirs Found in a Bathtub, 1973.
Cyberiad, 1974.
Futurological Congress, 1974.
The Investigation, 1974.
Star Diaries, 1976.
Mortal Engines, 1977.
Chain of Chance, 1978.
A Perfect Vacuum, 1978.
Tales of Pirx the Pilot, 1979.
Return from the Stars, 1980.
The Cosmic Carnival of Stanislaw Lem, 1981.
Memoirs of a Space Traveler, 1981.
More Tales of Pirx the Pilot, 1982.
His Master's Voice, 1983.
Imaginary Magnitude, forthcoming.

C. Nonfiction in Periodicals

"Promethean Fire" [Interview]. Tr. Yuri Sdobnikov. *Soviet Literature* 5(1968): 166–70.
"Ten Commandments of Reading the Magazines." Tr. Franz Rottensteiner. *Science Fiction Commentary,* no. 6 (1969), p. 26.
"Sex in SF." Tr. Franz Rottensteiner. *Science Fiction Commentary,* no. 3 (1970), pp. 2–10, 40–49.

"Poland: SF in the Linguistic Trap." Tr. Franz Rottensteiner. *Science Fiction Commentary*, no. 9 (1970), pp. 27–33.

"You Must Pay For Any Progress [Interview]. Tr. Franz Rottensteiner. *Science Fiction Commentary*, no. 12 (1970), pp. 19–24.

"Letter." *Science Fiction Commentary*, no. 14 (1970), p. 5.

"Unitas Oppositorum: The Prose of Jorge Luis Borges." *Science Fiction Commentary*, no. 20 (1971), pp. 33–38.

Review, *Robbers of the Future* by Sakyo Komatsu. Tr. Franz Rottensteiner. *Science Fiction Commentary*, no. 23 (1971), pp. 17–18.

"Lost Opportunities." Tr. Franz Rottensteiner. *Science Fiction Commentary*, no. 24 (1971), pp. 17–24.

"Robots in Science Fiction." Tr. Franz Rottensteiner. *Science Fiction: The Other Side of Realism*. Ed. Thomas Clareson. Bowling Green, Ohio: Bowling Green University Popular Press, 1971, pp. 307–25.

"Letter." *Science Fiction Commentary*, no. 26 (1972), pp. 28–30, 89–90.

"Letter." *Science Fiction Commentary*, no. 29 (1972), pp. 10–12.

"Culture and Futurology." *Polish Perspectives* 16, 1(1973): 30–38.

"On the Structural Analysis of Science Fiction." Tr. Franz Rottensteiner and Bruce R. Gillespie. *Science-Fiction Studies* 1, 1(1973): 26–33.

"Remarks Occasioned by Dr. Plank's Essay 'Quixote Mills'." *Science-Fiction Studies* 1, 2(1973): 78–83.

"The Time Travel Story." Tr. Thomas Hoisington and Darko Suvin. *Science-Fiction Studies* 1, 3(Spring, 1974): 143–54.

"An Interview with Stanislaw Lem" [Lem's English]. [Interview by Donald Say]. *Science Fiction Review* [Also cited as *Alien Critic*]. 3(August 1974): 4–15.

"Reflections for 1974." *Polish Perspectives* 17, 10(1974): 3–8.

"Todorov's Fantastic Theory of Literature." Tr. Robert Abernathy. *Science-Fiction Studies* 1, 4(1974): 227–37.

"Letter." *Science Fiction Commentary*, no. 41/42 (1975), pp. 90–92.

"In Response," *Science-Fiction Studies* 2, 2(1975): 169–70.

"Letter." *Science Fiction Commentary*, no. 44/45 (1975), pp. 96–97.

"Philip K. Dick: A Visionary Among the Charlatans." Tr. Robert Abernathy. *Science-Fiction Studies* 2, 1(1975): 54–67.

"SF: A Hopeless Case—With Exceptions." Tr. Werner Koopman. *Philip K. Dick: Electric Shepherd*. Ed. Bruce Gillespie. Melbourne, Australia: Norstrilia, 1975, pp. 69–94.

"Cosmology and Science Fiction." *Science-Fiction Studies* 4(1977): 107–10.

"Looking Down on Science Fiction: A Novelist's Choice for the World's Worst Writing." *Science-Fiction Studies* 4(1977): 126–27. Originally published in the *Frankfurter Allgemeine Zeitung*, February 22, 1975.

"In Response to Professor Benford." *Science-Fiction Studies* 5, 1(1978): 92–93.

"The Profession of Science Fiction: XV: Answers to a Questionnaire." Tr. Maxim and Dolores Jakubowski. *Foundation*, no. 15(1979): 41–50.

"Review of W. S. Bainbridge's The Space Flight Revolution." Tr. Franz Rottensteiner. *Science-Fiction Studies* 6, 2(1979): 221–22.

"Planetary Chauvinism: Speculation on the 'Others'." Tr. Franz Rottensteiner. *Second Look* 1, 10(1979): 5–9.

"The Future without a Future: An Interview with Stanislaw Lem." [Interview by Zoran Živiković]. *Pacific Quarterly* (Moana) 4(1979): 255–59.

"'. . . Knowing Is the Hero of My Books . . .'" [Interview by Andrzej Ziembiecki], *Polish Perspectives* 22, 9(1979):64–69.

"From Big Bang to Heat Death." Tr. Franz Rottensteiner. *Second Look* 2, 2(1980): 38–39.

"Letter." *Science Fiction Commentary*, no. 60/61 (1980), p. 4.

"A Conversation with Stanislaw Lem" [Interview]. *Amazing*, 27 (January 1981), pp. 116–19.

"Lem: Science Fiction's Passionate Realist" [Interview by Peter Engel]. *New York Times Book Review*, March 20, 1983, p. 7.

"Stanislaw Lem." *Contemporary Authors Autobiography Series*. Detroit: Gale, forthcoming 1984.

D. Excerpts (American and British)

"The 13th Journey." Tr. Harry Stevens. *The Modern Polish Mind*. Ed. Maria Kuncewicz. Boston: Little Brown, 1962, pp. 423–38. From *Star Diaries*.

"The Washtub Diary." Tr. Andrzej Konarek. *Polish Perspectives* 2(1964): 42–48. From "Introduction" in *Memoirs Found in a Bathtub*.

"The Computer Which Fought a Dragon." Tr. Krzysztof Klinger. *Polish Perspectives*, December, 1964, pp. 35–41. From *Bajki robotów*; in *Mortal Engines*.

"The Eighth Journey (From the Stellar Diaries of Ijon Tichy)." Tr. Andrej Konarek, *Polish Perspectives,* December, 1966, pp. 65–82. From *Dzienniki gwiazdowe;* in *Star Diaries.*

"The White Death." Tr. Michael Kandel. *Twenty Houses of the Zodiac.* Ed. Maxim Jakubowski. New English Library/Times Mirror, 1979, pp. 214–19.

"The Twenty-fourth Journey of Ijon Tichy," Tr. Jane Andelman; "The Computer that Fought a Dragon," Tr. Krzysztof Klinger; "The Patrol," Tr. Thomas Hoisington; and "The Thirteenth Journey of Ijon Tichy," Tr. Thomas Hoisington. *Other Worlds, Other Seas: Science Fiction Stories from Socialist Countries.* Ed. Darko Suvin. New York: Random House, 1970.

"Simon Merrill: Sexplosion." Tr. Andrzej Konarek. *Polish Perspectives* 14, 10(1971): 38–43. From *A Perfect Vacuum.*

"How the World Was Saved." Tr. Michael Kandel. *Antigrav.* Ed. Philip Strick. New York: Taplinger Publishing, 1976, pp. 27–31.

"In Hot Pursuit of Happiness." *View from Another Shore: European Science Fiction.* Ed. Franz Rottensteiner. New York: Seabury Press, 1973, pp. 3–50.

"Prince Ferrix and the Princess Crystal." Tr. Michael Kandel. *Literary Cavalcade,* April, 1977, pp. 41–45.

"Trurl's Machine." Tr. Michael Kandel. *Literary Cavalcade,* February, 1978, pp. 16–21.

"The Experiment." Tr. Michael Kandel. *New Yorker,* July 24, 1978, pp. 26–42. Published as "Non Serviam" in *A Perfect Vacuum.*

"Parisia." Tr. Michael Kandel. *New Yorker,* September 18, 1978, pp. 36–44. Published as "Gruppenfuehrer Louis XVI" in *A Perfect Vacuum.*

"Odds." Tr. Michael Kandel. *New Yorker,* December 11, 1978, pp. 38–54. Published as "De Impossibilitate Vitae and De Impossibilitate Prognoscendi" in *A Perfect Vacuum.*

"No Nonsense (Rien du tout, ou la conséquence)." Tr. Michael Kandel. *Encounter* 52, 4(1979): 3–7. From *A Perfect Vacuum.*

"The Test." Tr. Louis Iribarne. *Omni,* October, 1979, p. 86.

"The Albatross." Tr. Louis Iribarne. *Penthouse,* November, 1979, p. 150.

Return from the Stars. Tr. Barbara Marszal and Frank Simpson. *Omni,* June, 1980, p. 54.

"Metafantasia: The Possibilities of Science Fiction." Tr. Etelka de Laczay and Istvan Csicsery-Ronay. *Science-Fiction Studies* 8(1981): 54–71. From *Science Fiction and Futurology.*

"Phools." Tr. Joel Stern and Maria Swiecicka-Ziemianek. *New Yorker,*
October 12, 1981, pp. 42–48. "Twenty-fourth Voyage" from *Mem-*
oirs of a Space Traveler.
"Project Genesis." Tr. Joel Stern and Maria Swiecicka-Ziemianek.
New Yorker, November 2, 1981, pp. 48–53. "Eighteenth Voyage"
from *Memoirs of a Space Traveler.*
"The Washing Machine Tragedy." Tr. Joel Stern and Maria Swiecicka-
Ziemianek. *New Yorker,* November 30, 1981, pp. 44–53. From
Memoirs of a Space Traveler.
"Let Us Save the Universe." Tr. Joel Stern and Maria Swiecicka-Zie-
mianek. *New Yorker,* December 21, 1981, pp. 45–50. From *Mem-*
oirs of a Space Traveler.
"The Princess Ineffable" [from "The Tale of Three Story-telling Ma-
chines" in *Cyberiad*]: 96–99; "The Seventh Sally" [*Cyberiad*]:
287–94; and "Non Serviam" [*A Perfect Vacuum*]: 296–317 in *The*
Mind's I: Fantasies and Reflections on Self and Soul. Ed. Douglas
R. Hofstadter and Daniel C. Dennett. New York: Basic Books,
1981.
"The Man Who Invented Eternal Life." Tr. Joel Stern and Maria
Swiecicka-Ziemianek. *Penthouse,* January, 1982, pp. 122–28.
"Reminiscence II" from *Memoirs of a Space Traveler.*
"The Accident." Tr. Louis Iribarne. *Omni,* June, 1982, p. 50. From
More Tales of Pirx the Pilot.
"The Test." Tr. Louis Iribarne. *The Best from Omni—Number Three.*
New York: Omni, 1982: 28–35.

II. Material about Lem

A. Book Reviews Consulted

Blish, James. Review of *Solaris. Magazine of Fantasy and Science Fic-*
tion 40 (May 1971), pp. 42–43.
Lewis, Tom. Review of *Star Diaries. World Literature Today* 51 (Summer 1977), pp. 464–65.

Martin, George R. R. Review of *Return from the Stars*. *Book World*, June 22, 1980, p. 7.

Solotaroff, Theodore. *New York Times Book Review*, September 29, 1976, p. 1. Omnibus review.

Updike, John. Review of *Return from the Stars*. *New Yorker*, September 8, 1980, pp. 106–14.

———. Review of *Chain of Chance*. *New Yorker*, February 26, 1979, pp. 115–21.

B. Essays

Astle, Richard. "Lem's Misreading of Todorov." *Science-Fiction Studies* 2, 2(1975): 167–69.

Balcerzan, Edward. "Language and Ethics in Solaris." Tr. Konrad Brodziński. *Science-Fiction Studies* 2, 2(July 1975): 152–56.

Barnouw, Dagmar. "Science Fiction as a Model for Probabilistic Worlds: Stanislaw Lem's Fantastic Empiricism." *Science-Fiction Studies* 6(1979): 153–63.

Benford, Gregory. "On Lem on Cosmology and SF." *Science-Fiction Studies* 4, 3(1977): 316–17.

———. "Aliens and Knowability: A Scientist's Perspective." *Bridges to Science Fiction*. Ed. George Slusser, et. al. Carbondale: Southern Illinois University Press, 1980: 53–63.

Dick, Philip K. "The Lem Affair (Continued)." *Science-Fiction Studies* 5(1978): 84.

Dann, Jack, and Gregory Benford. "Two Statements in Support of Sargent and Zebrowski." *Science-Fiction Studies* 4(1977): 137–38.

Farmer, Phillip Jose. "A Letter to Mr. Lem." *Science Fiction Commentary*, 25 (December 1971), pp. 19–26.

Fogel, Stanley. "*The Investigation:* Stanislaw Lem's Pynchonesque Novel." *Riverside Quarterly* 6(1977): 286–89.

Guffey, George R. "The Unconscious Fantasy and Science Fiction: Transformations in Bradbury's *Martian Chronicles* and Lem's *Solaris*." *Bridges to Science Fiction*. Ed. George Slusser, et. al. Carbondale: Southern Illinois University Press, 1980, pp. 155–59.

Gunn, James. "On the Lem Affair." *Science-Fiction Studies* 4(1977): 314–16.

Hamling, William L. "The Editorial." *Imagination*, 4(May 1953), pp. 4–5.

Hofstadter, Douglas R. and Daniel C. Dennett, "Reflections." *The*

Mind's I: Fantasies and Reflections on Self and Soul. New York: Basic Books, pp. 99, 294–95, 317–20.

Jarzębski, Jerzy. "Stanislaw Lem, Rationalist and Visionary." Tr. Franz Rottensteiner. *Science-Fiction Studies* 4(1977): 110–25.

Kandel, Michael A. "Stanislaw Lem on Men and Robots." *Extrapolation* 14(1972): 13–24.

———. "On Translating the Grammatical Wit of S. Lem into English." Unpublished paper read before the American Association of Teachers of Slavic and East European Languages, 1974.

———. "Lem in Review (June 2238)." *Science-Fiction Studies* 4, 1(1977): 65–69.

Ketterer, David. "*Solaris* and the Illegitimate Suns of Science Fiction." *Extrapolation* 14(1972): 73–89.

Lavery, David L. " 'The Genius of the Sea': Wallace Stevens' 'The Idea of Order at Key West,' Stanislaw Lem's *Solaris*, and the Earth as a Muse." *Extrapolation* 21(1980): 101–05.

Le Guin, Ursula K. "European SF: Rottensteiner's Anthology, and the Strugatskys, and Lem." *Science-Fiction Studies* 1, 3(1974): 181–85.

———. "Science Fiction and Mrs. Brown" *Science Fiction at Large.* Ed. Peter Nicholls. London: Gollancz, 1976, pp. 31–32.

———. "Concerning the 'Lem Affair'." *Science-Fiction Studies* 4(1977): 100.

"The Lem Affair (Continued)." *Science-Fiction Studies* 5(1978): 84–87.

Lundwall, Sam J. *Science Fiction: What's It All About.* New York: Ace Books, 1971, pp. 233, 237–39.

Mullen, R. D. "I Could Not Love Thee Dear, So Much." *Science-Fiction Studies* 4(1977): 143–44.

Occiogrosso, Frank. "Threats of Rationalism: John Fowles, Stanislaw Lem, and the Detective Story." *Armchair Detective* 13(1980): 4–7.

Offutt, Andrew. "How It Happened: One Bad Decision Leading to Another." *Science-Fiction Studies* 4(1977): 138–43.

Potts, Stephen W. "Dialogues Concerning Human Understanding: Empirical Views on God From Locke to Lem." *Bridges to Science Fiction.* Ed. George Slusser, et. al. Carbondale: Southern Illinois University Press, 1980, pp. 41–52.

Purcell, Mark. "Lem in English and French. A Checklist." *Luna Monthly,* June, 1972, p. 11.

———. "Tarkovsky's Film *Solaris* (1972): A Freudian Slip?" *Extrapolation* 19(1978): 126–31.

———. "Filling the Void: Verne, Wells, and Lem." *Science-Fiction Studies* 8(1971): 134–41.

Rose, Mark. *Alien Encounters. Anatomy of Science Fiction.* Cambridge, Mass.: Harvard University Press, 1981, pp. 82–95, 157–65.

Rothfork, John. "Cybernetics and a Humanistic Fiction: Stanislaw Lem's *The Cyberiad.*" *Research Studies* (Washington State) 45(1977), pp. 123–33.

——. "Filling the Void: Verne, Wells, and Lem." *Science-Fiction Studies* 8 (1981): 134–41.

——. "Having Everything Is Having Nothing: Stanislaw Lem vs. Utilitarianism." *Southwest Review*, 66 (Summer 1981), pp. 293–306.

Rottensteiner, Franz. "Stanislaw Lem: A Profile." *Luna Monthly* December, 1971, p. 6.

Sargent, Pamela and George Zebrowski. "How It Happened: A Chronology of the 'Lem Affair'." *Science-Fiction Studies* 4(1977): 129–37.

Sargent, Pamela. "A Suggestion." *Science-Fiction Studies* 5(1978): 84.

Scarborough, John. "Stanislaw Lem." *Science Fiction Writers.* Ed. E. F. Bleiler. New York: Charles Scribner's Sons, 1982, pp. 591–98.

Scholes, Robert. "Lem's Fantastic Attack on Todorov." *Science-Fiction Studies* 2, 2(1975), pp. 166–67.

——. Structural Fabulation: *An Essay on Fiction of the Future.* Notre Dame, Ind.: Notre Dame University Press, 1975.

Scholes, Robert and Eric S. Rabkin. *Science Fiction: History. Science. Vision.* London: Oxford University Press, 1977, pp. 71, 84–85.

"Stanislaw Lem and the SFWA." *Science-Fiction Studies* 4(1977): 126–44.

Suvin, Darko. "The Open-Ended Parables of Stanislaw Lem and 'Solaris'," an Afterword in Lem's *Solaris.* Tr. from French by Joanna Kilmartin and Steve Cox. New York: Walker and Co., 1970, pp. 205–16.

——. "On the Poetics of the Science Fiction Genre." *College English* 34, 3(1972): 372–82.

——. "A First Comment on Ms. Le Guin's Note on the 'Lem Affair'." *Science-Fiction Studies* 4(1977): 100.

——. "What Lem Actually Wrote: A Philologico-Ideological Note." *Science-Fiction Studies* 5(1978): 85–87.

——. "Three World Paradigms for SF: Asimov, Yefremov, Lem." *Pacific Quarterly* (Moana) 4, 3(1979): 271–83.

——. "The Social Consciousness of Science Fiction: Anglophone, Russian, and Mitteleuropean." *Proceedings of the 7th Congress of the International Association of Comparative Literature.* Ed. M.

Dimic. Stuttgart: Bieber, 1979, pp. 537–41.
Szpakowska, Malgorzata. "A Writer in No Man's Land." *Polish Perspectives* 14, 10(1971): 29–37.
Theall, Donald F. "On SF as Symbolic Communication." *Science-Fiction Studies* 7(1980): 253, 256–61.
Thomsoen, Christian W. "Robot Ethics and Robot Parody: Remarks on Isaac Asimov's *I, Robot* and Some Critical Essays and Short Stories by Stanislaw Lem." *The Mechanical God.* Ed. Thomas P. Dunn. Greenwood, 1982.
Wilson, Reuel K. "Stanislaw Lem's Fiction and the Comic Absurd." *World Literature Today* 51(1977): 549–53.

III. Other Works Consulted

Ash, Brian. *Who's Who in SF.* New York: Taplinger Publishing, 1976, p. 136.
"Aus einem Interview mit Stanislaw Lem." *Quarber Merkur* 38(November 1974), pp. 20–35.
Balcerzan, Ewa. *Stanislaw Lem.* Waszawa: Pantstwowy Instytut Wydaniczy, 1973, pp. 175–78.
Geier, Manfred. "Stanislaw Lems Phantastischer Ozean." *Ueber Stanislaw Lem.* Ed. Werner Berthel. Frankfurt: Suhrkamp, 1981, pp. 96–163.
Robbe-Grillet, Alain. *For a New Novel.* Tr. Richard Howard. New York: Grove Press, 1965.
Rottensteiner, Franz. "Stanislaw Lem Bibliographie." *Quarber Merkur* 38(November 1974), pp. 68–81.
Rottensteiner, Franz and Klaus Staemmler. "Stanislaw-Lem-Bibliographie." *Ueber Stanislaw Lem.* Ed. Werner Berthel. Frankfurt: Suhrkamp, 1981, pp. 222–43.
Sila, Dominique. "Lems Spiele mit dem Universum." *Ueber Stanislaw Lem.* Ed. Werner Berthel. Frankfurt: Suhrkamp, 1981, pp. 52–67.
Suvin, Darko. *Encyclopedia of Science Fiction.* Ed. Peter Nicholls. New York: Branada, 1979, pp. 350–52.

————. "Stanislaw Lem." *Twentieth Century Science Fiction Writers.* Ed. Curtis C. Smith. New York: St. Martin's Press, 1981, pp. 620–21.

Turing, A. M. "Computing Machinery and Intelligence." *Computers and Thought.* Eds. Edward A. Feigenbaum and Julian Feldman. New York: McGraw-Hill Book Co., 1963, pp. 11–35.

Wiener, Norbert. *The "Human" Use of Human Beings: Cybernetics and Society.* Boston: Houghton Mifflin, 1950.

————. *Cybernetics: Or Control and Communication in the Animal and the Machine,* 2nd ed. Cambridge, Mass.: M.I.T. Press, 1961.

Index

177